THE ROLE OF INTELLECTUALS IN THE STATE-SOCIETY NEXUS

This strategic reflection was supported by:

NATIONAL INSTITUTE
FOR THE HUMANITIES
AND SOCIAL SCIENCES

Liliesleaf

A PLACE *Of* LIBERATION

THE ROLE OF INTELLECTUALS IN THE STATE-SOCIETY NEXUS

MAPUNGUBWE
INSTITUTE FOR STRATEGIC REFLECTION (MISTRA)

MAPUNGUBWE
INSTITUTE FOR STRATEGIC REFLECTION (MISTRA)

Mapungubwe Institute for Strategic Reflection (MISTRA)
First floor, Cypress Place North
Woodmead Business Park
142 Western Service Road
Woodmead 2191
Johannesburg

First published June 2016

© MISTRA 2016

ISBN 978-1-928341-03-1

Published by Real African Publishers
on behalf of the Mapungubwe Institute for Strategic Reflection
(MISTRA)

PO Box 3317
Houghton
Johannesburg 2041

Sub-editor: Barry Gilder
Copy editor: Angela McClelland

MAPUNGUBWE INSTITUTE (MISTRA)
[A NON-PROFIT COMPANY][104-474-NPO]
REGISTRATION NUMBER 2010/002262/08
["THE INSTITUTE"]

Contents

ACKNOWLEDGEMENTS

The Mapungubwe Institute for Strategic Reflection (MISTRA) expresses its deep thanks to the speakers, respondents and attendees at the roundtable that served as a basis for this publication. We thank the Liliesleaf Trust for partnering with us on this event and for providing their wonderful venue.

Warm thanks are also due to the staff of MISTRA and Liliesleaf who organised the roundtable and ensured its undoubted success.

Appreciation is also extended to Barry Gilder, who put this publication together, to Siphokazi Mdidimba who assisted with the sub-editing of the manuscript, and to Angela McClelland and Reedwaan Vally of Real African Publishers who copy-edited, designed and produced this publication.

MISTRA expresses profound gratitude to the donors who contributed to this project as well as those who have generally contributed to the work of the Institute.

CONFERENCE FUNDERS
National Institute for Humanities and Social Sciences
Liliesleaf Trust

MISTRA DONORS AND FUNDERS

Local Foundations and Trusts
First Rand Foundation
Nedbank Foundation
Oppenheimer Memorial Trust
Social Science Development Forum (SOSDEF)
Transnet Foundation

International Sources
Frierich-Ebert-Stiftung
People's Republic of China Embassy

Corporates
Absa
Anglo American
AngloGold Ashanti
Anglo Platinum
Aspen Pharmacare
Batho Batho Trust
Brimstone
Chancellor House
Discovery
Encha Group Limited
Kumba Iron Ore
MTN
Mvelaphanda Management Services
Naspers
Power Lumens Africa
Safika
Sanral
Sasol
Shanduka Group
Simeka Group
Standard Bank
Yard Capital Development Trust
Yellowwoods

Individuals
Robinson Ramaite
Thandi Ndlovu

Partners
National Advisory Council for Innovation (NACI)
Nelson Mandela Foundation
South African Reserve Bank
University of Johannesburg
University of Pretoria
University of South Africa
University of Witwatersrand

PREFACE

The very name of the Mapungubwe Institute for Strategic Reflection (MISTRA) expresses precisely the raison d'etre of the Institute – to encourage strategic reflection on the challenges facing South Africa, our region, our continent and the globe. There are many who seek to give blow-by-blow sound bites on events and issues of the day. Our focus is on taking the long, strategic view and drawing down from that the possible scenarios for tackling the problems of today as well as tomorrow.

In this spirit, MISTRA sees itself as encouraging a new intellectual movement in South Africa, one that to some extent at least sits back from the fray and provides independent, incisive, long-term thinking and analysis on where we have come from, where we are now and where we are going.

However, if we are to talk of a 'new' intellectual movement, the question is begged: what happened to the 'old' intellectual movement? What happened to the thinkers who inspired and led our struggle against colonialism, apartheid and exploitation? What has happened to the thinkers who gave substance and guidance and, in many cases, practical leadership to our attempts to undo the past and forge a new future?

In pursuit of answers to these questions, the Mapungubwe Institute, in partnership with the Liliesleaf Trust, hosted a roundtable in March 2015 on the theme *The Role of Intellectuals in the State-Society Nexus*. The roundtable received inputs from a range of thinkers, including Ibbo Mandaza, Ben Turok, Ari Sitas, Ayanda Ntsaluba, Xolela Mangcu, Joel Netshitenzhe, Tshilidzi Marwala and Nomboniso Gasa, as well as provocative and piercing inputs from the attendees.

This publication aims to put the inputs and debates at the roundtable further into the public domain and simply records the contributions of the main speakers, the respondents, as well as the discussion from the floor. The rigorous debate at the roundtable spilled out of the boundaries of the event itself and encouraged a number of thinkers to provide additional material for this publication – Z. Pallo Jordan, David Moore (with Tshilidzi Marwala), as well as Desiree Lewis.

On behalf of the MISTRA Board of Governors, I would like to express our profound thanks to the speakers and participants at the roundtable, to the trustees, management and staff of Liliesleaf, and to the management and staff of MISTRA who made the roundtable and this publication possible. We are also, of course, extremely grateful to the National Institute for the Humanities and Social Sciences (NIHSS) who made the event and publication possible and to all those donors who continue to support MISTRA. An intellectual movement needs not just intellectual resources, but more practical ones as well.

Professor Sibusiso Vil-Nkomo
Chairperson
MISTRA Board of Governors

INTRODUCTION

Historical Background

Throughout history, intellectuals have often played a key role in struggles for the modernisation of societies, national liberation and social justice. They have provided theoretical context, strategic (and sometimes tactical) guidance and, in many cases, themselves played a leadership and/or activist role. In South Africa, the history of the liberation struggle, especially from the late nineteenth century, is replete with efforts of the best intellectuals among the Black people and whites of conscience to conceptualise the cause of the liberation struggle and mobilise society against colonialism. These intellectuals drew inspiration from international experience and the lived experience and wisdom of various sectors of society. They also reproduced themselves through formal and informal educational initiatives.

In many cases, when political freedom is attained and social transformation begins, the intellectuals play a key role in envisioning the transformation, in policy formulation and in the political and administrative leadership of the new dispensation.

One of the greatest achievements of the struggle for national liberation in South Africa, and indeed the rest of the continent, was the lucidity with which African intellectuals analysed the manifestations of the systems they faced and articulated the post-independence ideal. In this way, they contributed immensely to the epistemology of the humanities and social sciences (HSS) on a global scale.

Post-independence Challenges

However, in many liberated nations the role of progressive intellectuals appears to diminish after a few years. In post-1994 South Africa, this can be attributed to a variety of factors, including:

- the devaluing of humanities and social sciences in the global era of narrow commercial economism, technicist approaches to the natural sciences and hyper-specialisation in centres of learning and the workplace;
- the absorption of many intellectuals into 'professional' party political

activity, as well as the state bureaucracy with its technical approaches and methodologies;

- the 'struggle' for material advancement among the emergent middle strata, which renders academic and intellectual pursuits less attractive; and
- populist degradation of the role of intellectuals in part of the public discourse, in an attempt, among others, to co-opt these intellectuals into a narrow factional loyalty.

These factors and the poverty of depth and relevance in the humanities and social sciences has had the effect of undermining the contribution that intellectuals are able to make to the complex processes of social transformation.

Widening Gulf

Arising out of all this, a gulf starts to develop between intellectuals and the political economic elites. Many intellectuals either conform to the dictates of the new socio-political environment out of the sheer pressure to maintain middle- and upper-class lifestyles, or concern themselves with mundane issues that do not advance society in any qualitative way. Others end up as shrill voices in the wilderness.

Some intellectuals do persist in the idealism that inspired the liberation struggle. In this context, they posit a systematic critique of what they perceive as inadequacies or failures of transformation policies and practices. Where applicable, they assert a principled belief that the vision, principles and ethics of the struggle are being compromised in actual practice. Partly as a result of this, as well as perhaps other factors, these 'struggle intellectuals' find themselves increasingly sidelined or 'purged' from circles of influence.

Intellectuals in Modernisation and Social Transformation

Yet, in human history, epochs of social transformation and modernisation have been anchored in profound intellectual engagement with critical questions of the day. Contestation around the re-ordering of social relations, idealism about technological advancements aimed at bettering the human condition, and the pursuit of philosophy and the natural sciences for their own sake – all these and other attributes have defined the renaissance of nations, regions and continents. During such epochs, the political and economic elites have either failed to contain the surge of 'enlightenment', or embraced it, thus catapulting nations to higher planes of social progress.

Where is South Africa located in all this? What is the place and role of intellectuals in the unfolding process of social change? Was the prominence of intellectual input into the strategic direction of society a unique character of the phase of resistance and the early period of transition to a democratic society? Is the current situation reflective of the 'normalisation' of society? What about the multitude of challenges that society faces which require ongoing theorisation? What is the role of intellectuals in the nexus between the state, the market and the citizenry?

These are some of the questions that the roundtable on *The Role of Intellectuals in the State-Society Nexus* and this publication sought to explore.

OPENING

Welcoming Remarks – Nic Wolpe

Good morning, ladies and gentlemen. Joel, MISTRA, thank you very much for agreeing to use Liliesleaf as a venue for what I consider to be an extremely important topic. I think it's very appropriate that this sort of discussion is taking place here at Liliesleaf because, on his last visit to Liliesleaf in July 2005, Nelson Mandela described what made Liliesleaf significant. He said that it was a place of discourse and engagement, and I think that's what it comes down to – discourse and engagement. The role of intellectuals within the liberation movement has a strong tradition of contributing to the liberation movement and its role.

I am actually at the moment reading the book on my father written by Steven Friedman and I was very interested where he highlights how the early works of my father stimulated a new paradigm, a new thought process that challenged traditional discourse and paradigm, and that's fundamental to the role of intellectuals. And I think that's one of the reasons why the ANC has been able to remain one of the oldest liberation movements on the African continent, because of the role intellectuals played within the movement.

I think it's also appropriate that it's taking place here as we mark the 60th anniversary of the adoption of the Freedom Charter, a document that, to all intents and purposes, has largely been forgotten and neglected because it has a very strong intellectual base, and it has, by its nature and content, stimulated debate and discussion within the ANC over the last 60 years in terms of some of the specific clauses and what they mean and how they talk to the current conditions of South Africa that we confront today.

So, in concluding, I would just like to say thank you very much and I hope that it is a very productive, useful and stimulating day.

Introductory Remarks – Mcebisi Ndletyana

Mine is an introductory role, to explain why we think this question is important to probe – the role of intellectuals in society. Interestingly, a journalist friend of mine, a couple of weeks ago when we got the invitation, called to ask why we thought it was important to probe the role of intellectuals when the country was faced with all sorts of problems: strikes, xenophobia, and all sorts of other things. My answer to him was that there are certain things that are secondary and there are some that are primary that have a permanent value. The role of intellectuals really has a permanent value because everything else that happens in society has to do, in most cases, with ideas and the role of intellectuals, especially in South Africa.

So the fact that we are probing this idea is not an anomaly, but it's something that we should have done a long time ago because intellectuals have been part of state formation, in South Africa especially.

Nationalism, especially in Africa, has primarily been an intellectual movement. Intellectuals led nationalist movements by virtue of their role in society. They were trained to lead society in that way, especially here during apartheid; during colonial society they went to mission schools and their role was really to mobilise the rest of society behind a colonial project. So, initially, they were recruited into the colonial project as intermediaries. For some time they did exactly that and their reward for mobilising society was equality. That was the idea, 'equality for all civilised men', as Cecil Rhodes put it. But in the 1890s or so, restrictions were imposed to limit the number of those who could vote and increasingly the franchise was denied to those who were 'civilised'. So from their role as mobilisers, to cultivate consent towards colonial conquest, they turned against colonialism and demanded equality for everyone else.

These were the folks who went on to form the African nationalist movement, primarily because the promise of equality had been betrayed by the English, especially, and they articulated – and this is one of the major, I think, achievements of African nationalists, or African intellectuals – the idea of equality. These were folks who really epitomised and believed in equality, racial equality, because they were essentially products of the meeting point between the Black and the white worlds. These were folks who really were raised to believe in the idea of equality, to believe that they were raised in the image of God.

When the English turned against equality and practised racism and thought of themselves as superior to Africans, these were the folks who reminded them of what they were saying and of what they termed the Christian ethic. They argued that to even believe in inequality is to betray the fact that perhaps Christianity was quite bankrupt within the white society, and they went on not only to preach the idea of equality, but to invent instruments, newspapers as well as organisations, to articulate and mobilise the rest of, not only the Black world, but the white world, about the importance and the value of equality.

So when we talk about intellectuals in South Africa, actually we are talking about folks who created the modern world through nationalism. So that's really part of the reason we are here; and secondly, society is not changed through singing and slogans – singing is quite popular these days – but society is changed through ideas; ideas that are articulated; ideas that are envisioned; ideas that are propagated through a whole lot of forums like this one, newspapers, etc. and for that you need intellectuals.

So that's partly the reason why we think it is important to gather here and probe this question. The only successful nationalist movement in Africa, so far, has been Afrikaner nationalism, interestingly, which invented Afrikaans and all sorts of things: mobilised Afrikaners behind their objective, achieved a breakthrough in 1948 and went on to create a modern state – in very awkward ways a successful state that we are now beginning, I'm told, to admit was not all so bad, yes, and there are certain things that they did which we need to emulate. That nationalism did not devour its own children after it achieved a democratic breakthrough and, yet, in the rest of Africa, all the intellectuals have been eaten up and they've left. I'm not sure what has happened to us. I'm not sure what is happening in Zimbabwe and the rest of the continent. Ibbo will tell us.

So the primary objective of why we are here is to probe how far we are in relation to that and how do we ensure, given the importance of the intellectuals' role in state making, how do we create the nexus between the intellectuals and the state because for the state to succeed it has to be led; it has to accommodate intellectuals. What we want to achieve has to be articulated; has to be thought out by intellectuals. We're not about creating an elitist movement, but nonetheless, ideas are quite important in enabling the masses to achieve their goals. Thank you.

PART ONE

The Intellect of Power and Power of Intellectuals in sub-Saharan Africa

The Role of Progressive African Intellectuals – Ibbo Mandaza

Some years ago, 1988 to be exact, we held a conference in Zimbabwe on the *Role of African Intellectuals in Society,* on the basis of which the main papers were published in a special edition of the *Southern Africa Political and Economic Monthly* (SAPEM Feb. 1988, No. 5). It was edited by Issa Shivji, and I quote an excerpt from his editorial entitled 'Soul- Searching':

> *These are times of crisis. Many an intellectual paradigm has crumbled as many a radical dream has crashed, particularly for radical intellectuals. For the intellectual of the status quo it hardly matters anyway. The ideals and examples from Mozambique to Vietnam that were held so dear in the 60's and the 70's have lost lustre and inspiration. Once unassailable citadels of theory are incessantly battered, occasionally sincerely but more often maliciously and in vengeance. In such times of crisis many things happen. Despair and dismay lead to spiritualism, if not cynicism. Worse, ranco[u]r replaces reason while treachery, rationalized as realism, goes unchallenged. Cowardice becomes respected as rational and practical, while commitment is considered unrealistic and puerile. But every cloud has a silver lining, as every process and movement is contradictory ...*

Then, Issa Shivji goes on to say (and this is for such intellectuals as Joel Netshitenzhe and myself, who had a stint in the state):

> *African intellectuals have been hitherto exceedingly mesmerized by the state, leading to being captured in state positions or alienated into inaction. Radicals among them have paid a lot of lip-service to the people and their causes but, in practice, have shown little faith in the*

same people. How else could one explain their practice, which in different circumstances and forms has been strikingly similar?

'It is in this light', Shivji concludes, that:

Intellectuals need to re-examine their past role over the last three decades of independence. Together with the revaluation of the post–independent policies and practices of the independent regimes, must go the revaluation and self-criticism of their opponents as well, particularly of those intellectuals who have claimed to espouse alternative policies and paths of development.

So what has changed since 1988? Clearly, Issa Shivji was describing a political landscape, which, at that time excluded southern Africa, even though Zimbabwe had completed eight years of independence. Therefore, his remarks, made as they were at a conference in Zimbabwe, could not have been oblivious of the failings of those intellectuals, such as myself, who had been members of the national liberation movement; who made bold declarations about a southern African exceptionalism in which, given the nature of the liberation struggle, neocolonialism was a remote possibility in Zimbabwe, Namibia and South Africa and, hardly a decade into post-independence, were lamenting the dream undone in *Zimbabwe: The Political Economy of Transition, 1980–86* (a book edited by myself but with contributions from a dozen of the country's leading intellectuals).

In many respects, therefore, the self-criticism and revaluation exercises had already begun in the case of some Zimbabwean intellectuals by the late 1980s, as evidenced by both the book referred to above and the conference on the *Role of Intellectuals in Society*. Here I want to reflect on some of the observations made then and, perhaps in the context of this discussion on South African soil, also on the role of progressive African intellectuals in the current conjuncture in which the former liberation movements, now in state power, exhibit the pitfalls no less problematic than their predecessors of the postcolonial state in Africa. Needless to add, the dilemma for progressive intellectuals – especially those in, or associated with, the state (as many of us are here) – is no doubt compounded and inherently complex.

Let's begin with some definitions of the intellectual, if thereby we also ensure that this intellectual has a dialectical relationship with the society in which he or she operates.

Ali Mazrui defines an intellectual as one who is 'excited by ideas and has acquired the ability to handle some of these ideas effectively'. Peter Anyang' Nyong'o states, in the same edition of *SAPEM* (1988), that:

> *An intellectual is a literate person who uses one's literacy to analyse systematically nature and society, or certain aspects of both, and present one's thoughts and ideas in coherent arguments or discourses that can make ordinary mortals understand how nature and society are constituted, why things happen the way they do, and what human beings can do to improve their lot and live much better than their predecessors did on this earth ...*

In other words, progressive intellectuals have always been concerned about change as espoused mainly in historical materialism; particularly change in the way society is organised towards revolution and progressive political, social and economic development.

And here I have to refer to two leading South African intellectuals who have had a profound influence on my own intellectual development: Archie Mafeje, especially his seminal piece on 'The Ideology of Tribalism', and Bernard Magubane and his famous article on 'Pluralism and Conflict Situations in Africa: A New Look'. And here I quote that profound line from Magubane, the methodology that distinguishes the progressive scholar from the rest:

> *The categories used to analyse society are important for they arise either from attempts to change the world or from attempts to resist that change.*

And, likewise, this very important one, as Magubane quotes from the French sociologist, Nicolaus:

> *The point is not to reinterpret oppression but to end it.*

So if we, as the school of progressive African intellectuals, stand out at all in this era, it is because of the extent to which we have sought to explain social reality and, in doing so, have contributed to the mission of the national liberation struggle in southern Africa: from the 'Dar es Salaam School' of the 1970s, including as it did such luminaries as Archie Mafeje, Claude Ake,

Okwudiba Nnoli, Arki Sawyer, Yash Tandou, Mahmoud Mamdani, Dani Nabudere, Samir Amin and Nathan Shamuyarira and, later, some of us, including those who gathered at the University of Zambia: Ben Turok, Jack Simons, etc. Not to forget the intellectual pillars of the struggle itself: Govan Mbeki, Joe Slovo, Ruth First and Pallo Jordan.

Then there was the African Association of Political Science (AAPS) that was formed in Dar es Salaam in 1973 and, likewise, the Council for the Development of Social Science Research in Africa (CODESRIA), which was inaugurated by Thandika Mkandawire and Abdallah Bujra in Dakar, Senegal, in 1978. Both bodies sought to mobilise and organise progressive African intellectuals across the continent and in the diaspora. Later, the Southern African Political Economy Series Trust (SAPES) was formed in Harare in October 1987 as a southern African expression of AAPS, and on the back of the monthly journal, *SAPEM*. For almost 30 years now, SAPES has been a rallying point for progressive intellectuals across the subregion and beyond, with a network of over 500 persons, numerous academic publications and monographs, as well as being the centre for intellectual discourse, training and conferences, including the Policy Dialogue Forum which is held almost weekly in Harare and hosts academicians and policymakers from across the subregion and beyond.

And today we are celebrating, through this conference, yet another forum of intellectuals on South African soil: the Mapungubwe Institute for Strategic Reflection (MISTRA), under the leadership of the likes of Joel Netshitenzhe and Barry Gilder, and people at this roundtable like Ayanda Ntsaluba and Xolela Mangcu.

So our efforts have been many and varied, but can we honestly say – and sometimes with misplaced arrogance – that African intellectuals have been at the centre of the processes that have seen southern Africa liberated, or mere appendages, and now unwitting participants in this animal that we call the postcolonial/post-apartheid state? And those of us who have been members of the national liberation movement, what has been our role in the period during which some of the militaristic and autocratic tendencies went unquestioned in the leadership of the movements themselves? Are we brave enough to establish, in retrospect and with the advantage of hindsight, the obvious correlation between the bad habits of the struggle days and those that characterise the leadership of the current state formations?

And now, confronted as we are in southern Africa by the political and economic pathology not dissimilar to that which we lamented with respect to the rest of Africa, how shall we confront the reality and proffer options and ways out of the crisis?

It is not enough to speak about the crisis without seeking to explain and dissect its causes. Perhaps there is general consensus amongst us here as to the nature and causes of this political and economic crisis. But then, what is the agency for change today?

Forty years ago, during the years of hope and optimism, the liberation struggle was the agency for change. Today, we are faced with three main challenges.

Firstly, the former liberation movements who constituted the anchor for the postcolonial/post-apartheid state have demonstrated a diminishing capacity for the agenda of economic transformation, let alone the basic requirements of the national democratic revolution. Herein lies the problem of the nation–state–in–the–making that Africa is saddled with today: the lack of an anchor class in the form of a national bourgeoisie around which to develop and strengthen it, economically and politically; the scourge of a new ruling class whose *raison d'etre* is a parasitic dependence on the state; a predatory state as the theatre for primitive accumulation, giving rise to a new class of a bureaucratic/state comprador bourgeoisie in partnership with their counterparts in the private sector, the merchants of BEE in South Africa or '10 per cents' in Zimbabwe; an incorrigible incumbency – to rule forever, at any cost, including institutionalised election rigging; a virtual securocrat state, as in Zimbabwe, with all the features that are inimical, contradictory and a denial of the national bourgeois democratic model.

Secondly, a disorganised civic society in the form of both the working class in particular but also the middle classes. Take Zimbabwe, for example: 50 per cent of all professional, intellectual and skilled persons are in the diaspora in South Africa, the subregion generally, in Europe, North America and in almost every part of the world. Can you imagine the impact of all this on civic society and the consequent incapacity to confront or even engage the state? Not to mention the negative effects on the economy. Likewise, in a country so de-industrialised as to have an estimated unemployment rate of 85 per cent, the working class has been eroded economically, socially and, therefore, also politically.

But the Zimbabwe scenario is now one likely to visit every other country in the subregion, including South Africa itself. Further north of us, we have the tragedy of African migration so magnified as thousands perish in the deserts and on the Mediterranean, fleeing from political and economic anarchy at home. 'Risking death in the Mediterranean: the least bad option for so many migrants', read a headline in the British *Guardian* newspaper the other day, quoting one of the migrants thus: 'It's the least worst option: a dead goat doesn't fear the butcher's knife.'

And how does this differ from the plight of African migrants in South Africa? Asks one newspaper:

> *They came to South Africa in search of a better life and, for a while, found the promised land ... The hunger, joblessness and poverty of their home in Zimbabwe was banished. Now the Chopos are among 3500 immigrants sleeping rough in crowded tents in heavily guarded transit camps, not in a Congolese or South Sudanese war zone but 21st century South Africa ... South Africa's reputation as a haven of tolerance for the tired, the poor, the huddled masses of a turbulent continent has been shaken: 'The fabric of the nation is splitting at the seams; its precious nucleus – our moral core – is being ruptured', quoting the Desmond and Leah Tutu Foundation.*

And then the answer from the wretched of the earth of South African society: 'The reason we're fighting foreigners is because of our government.'

So I repeat: what is the agency for change in this situation in which the postcolonial/post-apartheid state is so bereft of the capacity for autonomous and transformative economic development, and therefore given to underdevelopment, undemocratic tendencies and, in most cases, an unaccountable executive, a weak legislature, a pliant judiciary and distressed 'national' institutions?

In short, how do we, as progressive intellectuals respond to this African condition? It's a serious question: where do we look to? What shall we do beyond analysing and explaining the reality that confronts us today?

I have no ready answers, but I hope that this conference will be the beginning of a programme through which we can at least put these questions on the table and meet again, as your motto suggests: 'Galvanising intellectual resources in crafting strategic ideas and development options in pursuit of a better quality of life for all.'

First Response – Ayanda Ntsaluba

I'll be very brief. You know, when I was talking to some comrades some time back, and we were joking about something that used to happen in the camps in Angola (and some people might be familiar with this), every time there was a political discussion and somebody tried to be very smart, then somebody would say 'Remember Mark Shope, he said beware of the intellectuals'. Mark Shope was a respected senior comrade in the movement!

Now first of all, thanks Ibbo. It's always great to listen to you. I was just joking with Ibbo that, at some point when I was in Foreign Affairs during the difficult times in Zimbabwe, one of the things I used to really cherish were the opportunities to spend time with him in Harare and try to get some insights and understanding of what was going on in Zimbabwe at the time.

I've got a few things that I take out of Ibbo's input as well as the paper that he gave us, but also a few questions and some comments I would like to make.

The first thing that I really appreciated in the paper that Ibbo gave was, in a sense, the point about this current schizophrenic type of position that the radical African intellectual finds himself in. At one point he has got deep roots, deep roots of association, that were expedient to a large extent precisely because he needed to be authenticated by the Western progressives, but at the same time now wants to pull free of that influence and try to stand on his own as the authoritative voice essentially in trying to understand what's happening in the continent.

But actually I would argue that this schizophrenic behaviour, or this schizophrenic situation, is not only limited to that. You also have the same progressive African intellectual who prides himself or herself on having been a component part of the struggles for national liberation, who shaped and influenced that process, but somehow finds it very difficult at the same time to take responsibility for the missteps that have taken place.

We keep on asking the question: could the African intellectual have done something different and something better to make sure that some of the mistakes that we seem to continue to repeat from country to country actually would not be repeated? This then raises a very fundamental point to me, which is that – and Ibbo and Mcebisi referred to this – intellectuals essentially have the function of trying to inform public discourse. You inform public discourse during the time when the political establishment and the events that take place in a country represent the most noble in terms of the aspirations of the people, but then you are also supposed to shape and inform public discourse during the times when, in fact, the trappings of power get the better of us.

The key question that sometimes arises, certainly in the South African context – I'm sure in the southern African context – is why is it that, especially during the times when the trappings of power get the better of us, do we find it difficult to speak truth to power? Why is it that intellectuals find it very difficult to play the role that they are supposed to play?

Now in the extract that you referred to, Ibbo, you referred to the issue of whether this is cowardice; whether it is uncertainty. Is it perhaps the issue of old loyalties, loyalties that derive from the fact that actually we also were co-authors, to a limited extent, or to some extent, of both the positive and the negative narratives that we confront?

But I really think we need to reflect on that, because engaging that question will better provide us with the tools about the stance that we should assume as we move forward.

A related question, perhaps, is: is it not the case that during the struggles for national liberation right across our countries the people who rose to the top to lead were people who rose on account of their readiness to sacrifice? They rose because they were prepared to give everything in service of the people and of the nation. Maybe intellectuals found it very easy, given that type of political leadership, to be far more objective; to put their ideas on the table.

Given the changes that take place virtually in every country and the realities of power, is it not the case that somehow we might have idealised and therefore derived so much comfort from operating in the space where there's this significant alignment, alignment between leadership and service to the people, and now we suddenly stumble when we confront the realities of a rapidly changing situation?

Again, I think this, to me, is an issue. Unless we dispassionately confront, we are going to move in circles. Or else we will do what tends to be most comfortable in the circumstances, which is all of us quietly to withdraw and continue living our lives as normally as we can. But then, as we do that, we nonetheless carry the guilt, the guilt of betrayal, the feeling that actually we thought we wanted to do something better than simply living our lives.

The last point, Ibbo, that I wanted to raise, is the constraining effect of the dependence on external resources. This tends to be something that is recurring. The key question, for me, is the absence of a clear answer so many years post-independence. We need to chart a path that reduces the dependence on some of the institutions and our progressive Western sponsors if we want to assert the independence of the African intellectual.

Second Response – Xolela Mangcu

I won't repeat what the others have said about the importance of the topic of discussion. I will just say that there are probably as many definitions of the 'intellectual' as there are intellectuals. I was, however, delighted that Ibbo Mandaza cited Ali Mazrui's definition, which I first saw in Thandika Mkandawire's book on African Intellectuals. This is the idea of the intellectual as someone who is fascinated by ideas and taken up with their pursuit.

But the idea of the intellectual I want to suggest today comes from Michel Foucault. It is the idea of the intellectual as someone who problematises, who puts all certitudes under scrutiny, and for whom there are no holy cows. I choose this particular definition because it informs my approach to Ibbo Mandaza's paper.

Let me just start with what I think is the central premise of his paper. At the heart of it is a deeply felt concern about the hegemony of Western intellectuals in the interpretation of the African experience. But here is the irony. Inasmuch as African intellectuals lament white and Western scholars, they still tend to depend on analytic constructs that originated and were designed primarily for European societies. I have here in mind the twin culprits of Marxism and nationalism that inform radical political analysis.

The last time I looked, Marx was from Germany, and the last time I checked, much of what he was doing was writing about Europe and that's what really was at the forefront of his thinking as he developed his theory.

Equally problematic is nationalism, which too originated in late nineteenth century Europe. By that I mean the transformation of pre-existing concepts of the nation (or *natio* in Latin), which referred to small groups, or what we would today call ethnic groups, into larger national identities. Thus the Franks were, over time, able to dominate other regions to create French nationalism based mainly on the imposition of the language of one group of people onto the language of the nation. As Eugene Weber argues in *Peasants and Frenchmen*, not until the early twentieth century did the majority of the people of France see themselves as Frenchmen.

As electoral mobilisation began to take hold in Europe in the 1880s, different elites began to vie for control of entire national territories by appealing to glorious pasts. The historian Eric Hobsbawm describes these ideological appeals as forms of proto-nationalism. Hobsbawm described how this particular approach was inherited by people everywhere, including the so-called Third World. He notes that 'the leaders and ideologues of colonial and semi-colonial liberation movements sincerely spoke the language of European nationalism which they have so often learned from the West, even when it did not suit their situation'. Basil Davidson makes a similar point in another book called *The Black Man's Burden*. Hobsbawm continues to observe that '… as the radicalism of the Russian Revolution took over from the French Revolution as the main ideology of global emancipation, the right to self-determination, now embodied in Stalin's texts, henceforth reached those who had been beyond the range of Mazinni. Liberation in what was yet not known as the Third World was now everywhere seen as "national liberation" or, among the Marxists, "national and social liberation"'.

Stalin's famous definition, of course, was the idea that national groups shared a common history, culture and language. Nothing could be further from the truth, if one takes just the fact that the Berlin conference dismembered African societies and reconstructed them with no regard to such continuity.

The birth of nationalism explains why the South African Native Congress was formed in the 1880s – just after the formation of the Indian Congress in 1885. By the way, it is a fallacy to continue to insist that the ANC was born in 1912. The South African Native Congress formed in King Williams Town in the 1880s ultimately became the South African Native Convention in 1909 with the same set of characters involved. That meeting was attended by delegates from Natal, Transvaal, Free State and Botswana. The executive consisted of Rubusana (President), John Langalibalele Dube (Deputy President), Reverend Gabashane (Treasurer) and Allan K. Soga as Secretary. African dignitaries from around the country included Chief Silas Molema, Dr Abduraman of the African People's Organisation, and Chief Mehlomakhulu, with Dr Walter Rubusana as its President and John Langalibalele Dube as its Vice President. When Pixley ka Seme and his friends wrote the constitution of the ANC in their offices in 1911, they were doing so within the context of an already existing nationalist movement, which became the South African Native Congress under Kgobosana, and then, of course, the South African National Native Congress. It's an important point to make for two reasons: the first reason is that it was pointed out by S. E. K. Mqhayi in 1929, but nobody pays attention to people like Mqhayi because they exist outside of this discourse, this conceptual discourse of Marxism and nationalism that we've inherited from the West. S. E. K. Mqhayi pointed this out in 1929 when he rebuked R. V. Selope Thema's claim that the ANC was born in 1912:

This gentleman says that this assembly was founded by Dr Seme in 1912 … it is on precisely this point that I wish to enlighten this young man so that he sees his way clearly, because what he is focusing on is a worthy story indeed. As an old man I would like to take him back to the year 1887, the year of Thung'Umlomo, *'Stitch the Mouth'. In that year there was an effort here in the Cape to establish a major association with Mr Goda Sishuba in the chair and Mr JT Jabavu as secretary – but after a while Mr Thomas Mqanda became chairman and Mr Jonathan Tunyiswa secretary. That association was named the South African Native Congress* (Ingqungquthela).

However, I wish to use this example to highlight what happens when we preoccupy ourselves with European history as the basis of understanding ourselves. Finally, while I agree in principle that Western hegemony is a problem in the telling of the African narrative, I also want to caution against Manichean categorisations. The West, or what is now called the North, is full of African, African-American, Caribbean, Mexican, Indian thinkers who are conducting cutting-edge research on Africa with whom we should collaborate.

And finally, on the question of the role of intellectuals, I do not think intellectuals should necessarily be radicals or revolutionaries. As I said at the beginning, there are as many intellectuals as there are people. I teach a whole range of nineteen-year-olds whose parents send them to UCT not to become radicals, including some of you, right? I could not possibly say they do not have an intellectual role because they are not revolutionaries. That would be absurd.

So it seems to me that we have to disentangle the intellectual role from the national liberation movement. So there is a break that we have to make with our own history, even if we are going to reconnect with it. But the idea that we're going to forever depend on ideas and concepts that were originated at the end of the nineteenth century in Europe in perpetuity seems to me to be particularly problematic. Thank you.

Discussion

Hassan Lorgat:

We work with communities surrounding the mines. From Ibbo's talk he seemed to speak about state-centric concentration of intellectuals. But the state itself has been captured over the years by big business and many of the liberation stalwarts became apologists for a system that excludes many people. So the kind of work we do is to get poor people to talk for themselves, which these forums do not allow.

For example, the names Ibbo mentioned of historical activists, I don't think he mentioned one woman's name. So I think that the role of intellectuals is to question some of them. They're not necessarily the ones that will side with you, but the intellectuals we're talking about here are those who are largely on the side of the people, the marginalised. So Ibbo, I think that there's been a total disregard of poor people and an increasing marginalisation of working-class people in the discourse.

Mohamed Motala:

I work for an organisation called the Community Agency for Social Enquiry. My point is similar to what Hassan is saying. None of the speakers identified the role of intellectuals in activism, and I think that historically, when intellectuals were involved directly with organisations that were organising people, then change, and the potential for change, was much clearer.

David Maimela:

I have two comments. The first one relates to the urge to want to define what an intellectual is. I really think that, just like beauty, there is no one definition for an intellectual. However, you can talk of intellectual work. I'm saying this because you look at the works, for instance, of Miriam Makeba; you look at the works of Oliver Mtukudzi – that's intellectual work, right? Intellectual work is not produced into the formalistic scholarly written work that you find in books. How do you think poor people, who are in the majority in this world, survive through their daily lives? How do they survive poverty if they do not apply themselves?

The second point is a brief one. I really do not think that nationalism, nationalist consciousness and nationalist sentiment are European concepts. I think they have always existed before the Berlin Conference.

Sibusiso Vil-Nkomo:

One comment on the issue of intellectuals. I'm always reminded of the work by Professor Mkandawire who did an analysis of the late President Kwame Nkrumah. He stated that Nkrumah was a politician, philosopher, intellectual and leader of his community. Unfortunately, he was his own intellectual advisor, political advisor and economic advisor, and most likely he was advising himself also about how Ghana should pursue its development trajectory.

The second point I want to make very quickly is, I don't think, Ibbo, we have answered the question of why our universities exist and what are the relevant and substantial contributions our South African intellectuals must really make in South Africa as a so-called 'developmental state'.

And lastly, you spoke about the political economy and the political kingdom versus economics. You are right: seeking the political kingdom is not a condition sufficient enough to develop a country like South Africa. What is interesting with this is that, when some of us studied economics and came back to this country, we knew that the political kingdom would sooner than later be confronted with the realities of not influencing the economy. We got lost in the political kingdom and the public service. We ended up not studying and analysing economics: from urban and regional economics, rural economics, economics of poverty and discrimination, public sector economics and agricultural economics.

Ibbo Mandaza Responds:

Thank you to the respondents who have put a new dimension, and therefore I want to answer the questions raised in three ways. The first is really to agree on the definition of intellectual, that, as Xolela said, there are as many as there are intellectuals, the broadest of course being that any literate person is an intellectual. I agree that in much of our discourse as intellectuals we have been rather incestuous over the years. There are certain assumptions we make about ourselves, but we are broadly people who are devoted to political economy. And even if it is true that Marxism has European roots, it purports to be a science, and I can't think of a better methodology in explaining social reality. I think we should see this as part of human history where certain ideas come up, rather than allocate them to a continent.

I think clearly that the political economy approach is an important one and it's a method that we have used in teaching as scholars. It's probably the best so far in explaining social realities.

The second, of course, is the point I want to make that, yes, we have the burden of history. We fought against imperialism and colonialism and yet we are products of the same. It's a fascinating dialectic with reality. We purport to be new in terms of our pursuit of development, and yet we're not so new. And by the way, nationalism is as old as class: nothing new, not European at all. When you have the notion of class, class rule, class domination, which is as old as humanity, from the days of primitive communalism, right down to feudalism, to capitalism, the notion of nation, territoriality is defined around an anchor class. And nationalism, really, if we have to go back in European history, goes back to the Westphalian state and the origins of the bourgeois state, which is a model, willingly or unwillingly, that we are following.

We may have a bourgeois state in Africa without a bourgeoisie, but it's a bourgeois state, which is a pragmatic that we have to examine. If we follow the tendencies of a bourgeois state, should we be judged on the basis of the extent to which we adhere to it? I believe that when you talk about a non-democratic state you are actually *ipso facto* applying the criteria of the bourgeois state.

If we do accept – as it appears that we have – a parliament based on the Westminster model, shouldn't we be judged on the basis of that?

The more vexing question is precisely this: can a bourgeois state model thrive where there is no national bourgeoisie? Secondly, is it possible to create a national bourgeoisie? The concept in your discourse in South Africa, the concept of national democratic revolution – have you arrived? What does it mean? That's precisely the idea of a national bourgeois model, even though Joe Slovo did not say it in those terms. And when Thabo Mbeki a few years ago dabbled with the idea that we need the national bourgeoisie in South Africa by merging the existing white bourgeoisie with an emergent Black bourgeoisie – is it called BEE or something? Well, it has failed. Sami Anood said it is impossible to create a national bourgeoisie in the area of international capital. So what is the option? Corporate bourgeoisie or the SADC states that our states have become in southern Africa? We are SADC states but basically all we are doing is law and order and facilitating the pillaging of our countries in which many of us are involved as comprador bourgeoisie. I will stop there. That's the problematic.

Xolela Mangcu Responds:

First of all, I agree entirely with the idea of intellectuals who've always worked with movements as part of the range of affiliations that intellectuals have had; some have worked with movements, some have not.

I do have an issue with Neville Alexander – I'm actually writing a chapter for a book about him – particularly his refusal to accept the ontological dimensions of people's realities on the basis of his assertion that they are not scientific and they are not based on scientific class analysis. I have the greatest respect for Neville; I know he worked with communities, but he could only go so far, and on the issue of race, for example, I have some serious disagreements with him.

So I agree with you, he was an engaged intellectual. I like that term. I think it's C. Wright Mills' term, the idea of the engaged intellectual, that I like more than Gramsci's notion of the organic intellectual, and that takes me to the issue of whether we can define an intellectual.

I don't think everybody is an intellectual. That's where I differ from Gramsci. I am an intellectual. For the past twenty years I've been calling myself an intellectual and I'm not going to stop until I die.

To talk about intellectual work and not deduce that the person who does that is an intellectual seems a little tricky for me. The person who does whatever you call intellectual work is for me an intellectual, and we should claim that identity for people in just the same way as when somebody says I'm a business person or I'm a sportsperson or I'm a politician. We don't question everything else except this one term and we have to ask ourselves why is it – particularly Black people – why do we question ourselves when we call ourselves intellectuals?

But let me respond to the issue of nationalism and nationality. There is a big difference between nationality and nationalism. What you are talking about, David and Ibbo, is a very important distinction. In the history of the formation of the nation, the idea of the nation to begin with, the idea of people imagining themselves as belonging to one country, one kind of national territory, the idea of people organising themselves on the basis of those imaginings into a state, that is nationalism.

So nationalism is a political phenomenon that comes only into being when people claim a particular nationality, on whatever they base it. Many people claim it on some kind of cultural past, on some kind of historical past, but some people, particularly in South Africa, we claim it basically on what it is that you can make of the nation. In other words, the nation is not based on any proto-nationalist idea.

Now the proto-nationalist idea is the idea of nationality; it's the idea that there is a group of people who belong to one nation. That is not in dispute. But nationalism is a different political concept and phenomenon and that phenomenon comes into place when you move away from what one calls the threshold principle. In other words, whatever works, whatever we imagine ourselves to be, that's a nation. But in the late nineteenth century that particular idea takes on particular ethnic and linguistic dimensions that led to Stalin giving us his description of the nation, which is a form of nationalism.

Finally, a point that I want to make with respect to what Ibbo was saying has to do with the issue of the universities. It seems to me that it's very important, Ibbo, that instead of focusing on individual scholars, the question we have to ask ourselves is: what is the institutional challenge? Unless you address that challenge, as a country or as a continent, you will continually be faced with the problem you were talking about. In other words, we won't have the strength to engage with these European or Western or Euro-modernist intellectuals you were talking about, because you're always operating from a position of weakness.

And so it seems to me that, if there's one thing we really have to think about in this country, it is the idea of what the institutional prerequisites are that we need to produce intellectuals in Africa and in South Africa. You have a government that spends billions of rands on consultants, and who are those consultants? White folks. The very white folks that they lament by day, they enrich by night.

And finally, we must get away from the idea that the political party is the essence of all intellectual work and wisdom. I mean, there was pretence about that when President Mbeki was president, but it has become laughable now with Jacob Zuma. So let us dispense with the idea that the political party is the basis of where intellectuals and real intellectual work actually takes place.

Ayanda Ntsaluba Responds:

Just two points. When we talk about intellectuals, they are not a homogeneous group to begin with and some people would even categorise them as loyalists, reformist or radical.

The second point is whether, as you talk about the tension that exists between Western and African intellectuals, or schools of thought, the one can exist without the other. I think it's also important to bear in mind that broadly human historical progress has to be based on taking the best out of different regions, continents, religions and cultures. So what we should always try to avoid is to think that anything African has to be conceptualised right from the beginning. I think the acid test, for me, is always the issue of whether we can indigenise concepts and ensure that they actually correlate to the reality of people, especially if we use as a starting point that the role of intellectuals essentially is about facilitating an informed public discourse. If that is the case, then part of the advantage that those who call themselves intellectuals have, is to pull from a wide variety of ideas and thoughts and try to synthesise those and make them relevant to the reality of people where you are operating.

PART TWO

Theorising the South African Renaissance Ideal

Theorising the South African Renaissance Ideal –
Joel Netshitenzhe

Introduction

Without entering the debate about definitions of intellectual work, and what Professor Thandika Mkandawire refers to as 'quintessentially the labour of the mind and soul',[1] I wish to posit an extension of the historical context by arguing that intellectual work preceded colonial conquest.

Needless to say, precolonial society in its various strands had an intellectual organising framework that defined sets of beliefs, artistic expressions, rationalisation of systems of social organisation and abstract intellectual pursuits. It can be argued that, from the artisans, traders, poets, generals, spirit mediums and administrators of Mapungubwe to Autshumao, Makhanda, Moshoeshoe's counsellors and Ntshingwayo (one of Cetshwayo's commanders), these intellectuals were critical in preserving, sustaining and advancing culture in the broad sense.

Historical Breaks and 'Modernity'

This issue is canvassed not for purposes of glorifying the past, but to acknowledge it; and primarily in order to draw attention to the transition that African societies endured as a consequence of colonial subjugation. Along with that was the imposition of Western education and a form of 'modernity' – in the less pejorative sense, pertaining to the introduction of advanced productive forces and the emergence of a modern, albeit colonial, state. This is important because, in theorising the South African renaissance ideal, we cannot ignore the persistence of some form of indigenous knowledge and, critically, the break that was imposed on the evolution of

African societies.

However, such breaks are not unique to colonial experiences. The Meiji restoration[2] of nineteenth century Japan was a self-imposed economic, social and political transformation of Japanese society. The same can be said about the emergence of the State of Qin[3] some 2,500 years ago, and later the 'four modernisations' of Zhou Enlai and Deng Xiaoping,[4] and the European Renaissance that started about 700 years ago. The East Asian transformations, in particular, reflected, among others, a profound and brutal self-critical paradigm based on an appreciation of the deficits (or what some of them called 'backwardness') in national development, and a determination to rise from the pain and shame of national humiliations. This paradigm is largely absent in South African (and to a significant extent, African) intellectual and socio-political discourse.

The break in the social evolution of indigenous South African communities, as a consequence of colonialism, means that an imposed alien modernity required of the subjects to remake themselves in the image of the colonial masters. From language to world outlooks, a psychology could easily set in always to seek affirmation and reassurance from the very colonial masters. On the other hand, the tools of an imposed modernity could be remoulded into weapons of struggle in the hands of the oppressed. In that sense, the colonialists became 'an unconscious tool of history'.[5] It is in the tortuous effort to find a resolution between these contradictory states that sovereign South African (and African) intellectual pursuits should determine their fulcrum.

And so, theorising the South African renaissance ideal should transcend the mindset to inherit, maintain and somewhat tinker with the socio-economic pillars of the status quo ante. To quote David Scott, the subalterns should not perceive of themselves as '... passive objects of a dominant civilizational power, merely assimilating or mimicking Europe, but rather [as] self-conscious actors, resisting, translating, displacing, and so on, that dominant power in the course of making their own history'.[6]

Two strands of thought therefore inform one's approach to the notions of renaissance, civilisation and modernity in the South African context. The first is about the agency of resistance and reconstruction as propagated by luminaries such as W. E. B. du Bois, Pixley ka Isaka Seme, Kwame Nkrumah, Sheikh Anta Diop and Thabo Mbeki. The second derives from an understanding of civilisation as a progressive improvement in the mastery of nature and pursuit of humane sociopolitical relations. When Biko and Seme argue that Africa can give 'the world a more human face' by introducing a civilisation that is 'humanistic ... moral and eternal',[7] they thus introduce a fundamentally important quality to the conceptualisation of civilisation and renaissance.

Renaissance Ideal in Evolution

In this year of the 60th anniversary of the Freedom Charter,[8] it is perhaps apposite to locate the discussion on the South African renaissance ideal in the provisions of, and debate around, the Charter. But before this, some brief observations about the preceding historical period deserve reflection.

The first issue relates to the stature of political leadership. There is no doubt that the liberation ideal owes much of its conceptualisation to the African intellectual traditions that started to emerge in the mid-nineteenth century. What is of utmost importance to our discussion is that it was the best from within this community that took up the cudgels in articulating the collective dreams of the oppressed. Besides their intellectual prowess, they were community leaders in their own right and, as much as humanly possible, the paragons of virtue. This ensured that they commanded respect beyond the narrow constituency of political activism.

The second observation is about the question posed earlier regarding the image of the colonial masters constituting the canvas upon which even the notions of liberation are defined. It is a matter of historical record that, in the first two decades of the existence of the African National Congress (ANC), its leadership campaigned for a qualified franchise. This did not necessarily reflect an ideal inferior to what obtained for the white community – which itself had qualifications pertaining to literacy and assets. Yet this approach persisted even after 'qualifications for the white franchise' were removed in 1931:[9] more a reflection of appeasement so whites would not feel overwhelmed by the Black masses. For the record, it was the Communist Party of South Africa (CPSA), which as early as the 1920s pioneered the demand for universal franchise in a Black republic.

By the 1940s this had changed with the 1943 African Claims adopted by the ANC calling for 'the extension to all adults, regardless of race, of the right to vote and be elected to parliament, provincial councils and other representative institutions'.[10]

What is striking in the African Claims is the attention paid to social issues, including such matters as free and compulsory education, free medical and health services, as well as collective bargaining and insurance for workers. But aside from demands for 'an equal share in all the material resources of the country', including 'fair distribution of the land', 'equal opportunity to engage in any occupation, trade or industry' and 'recognition of the right of the Africans to freedom of trading', the *African Claims* document was quite sparse on matters to do with equitable distribution of wealth.

The Freedom Charter thus represented a major advance in these and other respects.

Reflections on the Charter Ideals

The aim here is not to conduct a comprehensive analysis of the Freedom Charter, but to identify a few issues in its provisions for debate.

In reiterating the self-evident truth that government and state legality and legitimacy should derive from the people as a whole, and that 'South Africa belongs to all who live in it', the Freedom Charter asserts a profound and abiding non-racialism and democratic bent. Further, the Charter's progressive nature lies in its recognition of the intertwining of racial oppression and economic exclusion. Thus, its ringing injunctions on the reordering of wealth distribution, including land, stand out as a towering monument to the ideals of social justice.

Among others, three critiques have been proffered on the Charter's starting point on these issues.

The first is about what some interpret as the equation of oppressor and oppressed. But could South Africa have developed a different approach, given the 'colonialism of a special type' in which the large settler community had made the country their permanent home? What has not found resonance in discourse on this issue, though, is the responsibility on the part of beneficiaries of apartheid colonialism, in practical material terms, to contribute to the righting of the historical injustice. Proposals such as the TRC recommendation on a wealth tax and once-off levy on corporate and private income were not sufficiently debated. The 'fight back' of the first decade of freedom resulted in a conceptual stalemate; and efforts such as the Business Trust initiative petered out. The notion that current privilege has little to do with the apartheid order of things is bandied about as fact. An opportunity was missed and resentment will persist.

The second critique relates to the Freedom Charter's reference to 'all national groups', and thus an implied subtraction from the principle of individual rights. This is also criticised as undermining solidarity among Black people who were all victims of oppression. However, besides the issue of oppressor and oppressed canvassed above, is the recognition of apartheid's hierarchy of oppression among Black people themselves a conceptual aberration, or does it enjoy resonance in lived experiences – thus requiring careful management in policy and practical programmes?

The third critique derives from a rejection of the notion of 'colonialism of a special type' that would require the creation of a national democratic society as the maximum programme of the ANC. According to one of these critiques, the South African social system could be characterised as 'racial capitalism' – with race and class so intertwined that the antagonisms could only be resolved through the creation of a socialist order as an immediate objective. It can be argued that this approach underplays not only the principle of broad fronts and the variety of interests that coalesced in the liberation alliance, but also the array of class forces on a global scale.

Yet, a retort about society's experiences since 1994 – with current levels of poverty and inequality defined mainly along racial, gender and spatial lines – would be thoroughly justified. In this regard, the issue may not be so much about building a socialist system, but about the radical nature of socio-economic policies that have been implemented since the advent of democracy. Is it in fact possible to build 'non-racial capitalism' when the odds have historically been so heavily stacked against Black people?

This brings us to the debate about the interpretation of the property question as articulated in the Freedom Charter; in particular, the central injunctions that the 'mineral wealth beneath the soil, the banks and monopoly industry shall be transferred to the ownership of the people as a whole' and 'restrictions of land ownership on a racial basis shall be ended, and all the land redivided amongst those who work it to banish famine and land hunger'.[11] The word 'interpretation' is used deliberately because it has a subjective premise, and assumes tints in the eye of the beholder. In this regard, context becomes crucial so as to avoid games of make-believe and taunts and ripostes that are more about public political postures than the science of social development.

What are some of these postures? To paraphrase, these are, firstly, that the Charter did not intend nationalisation and those who assert the opposite are distorting the thinking of the drafters. The second approach is the inverse of the above, with accusation that the post-apartheid government has betrayed the ideals of the struggle. The third one evades the issue and resorts to listing finicky detail about Black Economic Empowerment, the Minerals and Petroleum Resources Development Act and a state mining company, as well as poorly implemented land restitution and redistribution as proof that the Charter is being meticulously implemented.

None of these approaches helps the discussion much, for each one of them tends to ignore context. When Nelson Mandela argued in the 1950s that 'in demanding the nationalisation of the banks, the gold mines and the land, the Charter strikes a fatal blow at the financial and gold-mining monopolies and farming interests that have for centuries plundered the country and condemned its people to servitude',[12] he was accurately reflecting the generally understood meaning of the Charter's property clauses then. This is reiterated in the ANC Strategy and Tactics document adopted at the Morogoro Consultative Conference in 1969.[13]

Such was the interpretation of the Charter when state ownership was seen as the primary instrument through which redistribution of wealth and economic leadership could be exercised. And this was 'within an international context of transition to the Socialist system, of the breakdown of the colonial system as a result of national liberation and socialist revolutions, and the fight for social and economic progress by the people of the whole world'.[14]

The approach in this regard has changed. And this is not merely on account of a changed global environment, but because of a different approach to the role of the state in economic development, with the need or otherwise of state ownership weighed on a case by case basis. To quote from the ANC's 1992 *Ready to Govern* document:

> *The primary question … is not the legal form that state involvement in economic activity might take at any point, but whether such actions will strengthen the ability of the economy to respond to the massive inequalities in the country, relieve the material hardship of the majority of the people, and stimulate economic growth and competitiveness.*
>
> *In this context, the balance of the evidence will guide the decision for or against various economic-policy measures. Such flexibility means assessing the balance of the evidence in restructuring the public sector to carry out national goals. The democratic state will therefore consider:*
> * *Increasing the public sector in strategic areas through, for example, nationalisation, purchasing a shareholding in companies, establishing new public corporations or joint ventures with the private sector;*
> * *Reducing the public sector in certain areas in ways that will enhance efficiency, advance affirmative action and empower the*

historically disadvantaged, while ensuring the protection of both consumers and the rights and employment of workers.

Such a mixed economy will foster a new and constructive relationship between the people, the state, the trade union movement, the private sector and the market.[15]

In other words, government is implementing a specific interpretation of the Freedom Charter from the point of view of the current logic on the role of the state in economic development. It may not articulate this clearly, or it may be implementing this badly, but this does not necessarily mean that the approach itself is misplaced. It may well be that a different logic is required, and other approaches may produce better results. But an argument to this effect would have to demonstrate whether principles in the current logic are in fact being implemented, effectively and to the letter, or whether the problem lies elsewhere!

The changes envisaged in the Freedom Charter, the framework of which is captured in the country's Constitution – encompassing all generations of human rights – imply a fundamental transformation of apartheid political and social relations; in other words, a Revolution. To argue that the 'South African Constitution … provides for transformation and not a radical revolution'[16] is therefore incorrect, and reflects an aversion to what, for instance, the Americans and the French have embraced as a proud part of their being.

Precarious Elements in the Current Conjuncture

Recent events have thrown up contradictory trends about the state of South Africa's polity and its prospects going forward. On the one hand, the overwhelming majority of South Africans have, broadly, shown support for the National Development Plan and a yearning for social compacting to realise a better life for all. On the other hand, negative events – ranging from the Marikana tragedy to increasingly violent local protests, disruptions in the legislatures, shoddy responses to injunctions of institutions such as the Public Protector, and strange developments in state institutions – do pose a question about the sturdiness of the country's constitutional order.

Against the backdrop of these developments are the recent electoral outcomes, which reflected, among others, the following trends:[17]

- the persistence of race as a marker of political self-interest, with close to 100% of whites voting for the Democratic Alliance (DA) and one or two smaller parties that have historically been associated with privileges of the colonial order, and increasing numbers from within the Coloured and Indian communities associating themselves with these schools of thought – and ditto with the African community in relation to the ANC and 'liberation parties', though there is greater diversity within this community in terms of electoral choices;

- the recession of ethnic identity and regionalism within the African community, with the three largest parties having a national footprint, and KwaZulu-Natal attaining averages similar to other provinces in terms of African support for the ANC (with indications that the latter is largely premised on actual 'service delivery' in deep rural parts of the province);
- the continuing loss of support by the ANC (since 2009), especially in most of the Metros, with indications of a rising prominence of concerns around issues of ethics, especially among sections of the African middle strata who are starting to evince a fickleness typical of those who are less dependent on state largesse; and
- the shift in support for parties that profess 'radical' approaches on socio-economic issues such as nationalisation and land redistribution without compensation – which, since 1994, had collectively gained barely above one per cent of the vote, now attaining some six per cent.

Are these issues at all related, and what is their relevance to the theorisation of the South African renaissance ideal?

At the root of many of these developments is the persistence of exclusion and marginalisation reflected in high levels of poverty, and the growing inequality in society, especially within the African majority (as distinct from across the various racial groups). The class composition of society is changing with larger numbers of Black people ascending to the status of 'middle class'; educational attainment among them is also on the rise. At the same time, social status is still defined mainly by race, with a sediment of society – particularly young people, women and rural communities – intensely marginalised from meaningful economic activity.

While its character (e.g. levels of education) and absolute numbers may have changed, this 'underclass' has always been there during the past 21 years. And so, why is this social tinder now more prone to catching fire? The answer lies in the balance between hope and despair.

When the structural nature of South Africa's unemployment problem combines with rising inequality, consequences of a global recession, persistence of 'racial capitalism' and signs of advancement among a few from within the previously disenfranchised, the social tinder becomes even more flammable. But it is in more than the objective circumstances that we should seek answers – for again, many of these circumstances have been with us during the past 21 years.

When weak state capacity merges with gross manifestations of corruption at local level (of the Mothutlung/Brits type where water infrastructure was deliberately sabotaged so local politicians and bureaucrats could make money with water tank vendors), the sense of hope loses its flicker. In the place of political persuasion and infusion of hope, state security agencies become the first and last line of defence, and some communities start deliberately to target these agencies when they engage in protest. When media reports and commentary on government are replete with cases of abuse of state resources, a sense of impunity, manifestations of patronage on a grand scale in state-owned enterprises, and strange shenanigans in critical state agencies, the very legitimacy of the state and the democratic order at large are severely undermined.

In other words, rulers themselves can, by commission or omission, create conditions for a chain of de-legitimisation that may start off with the individual leader, extending to the party, the government and ultimately the state and the polity as a whole. In some postcolonial societies on the African continent, it was precisely at such moments that the Right and the self-declared Left found common cause to revolt against the status quo, with the military forces taking advantage of the situation to stage coups d'état. This, however, is not possible in South Africa. Yet, in other instances on the continent, the state started to rely more and more on overt and/or covert acts of repression.

And so the chain of de-legitimisation takes various forms, with those who are exploiting both the social tinder and the subjective weaknesses aiming to displace the ruling party in the polls. On the extreme, the state is goaded to take precipitate action, such as in the Marikana tragedy and recently in the disruptions in Parliament, which action in turn aggravates the process of de-legitimisation. Elements of the Right also seize on the opportunity and strange alliances take shape. The more extreme among these elements – particularly rabid racists who had gone into hibernation – come out of the woodwork and latch onto this to question the very capacity of Black people to govern, and to rationalise latent disloyalty to the new dispensation.

Parallels, in this regard, can be drawn in relation to the unseemly squabbles in the Congress of South African Trade Unions (Cosatu). A comprehensive analysis of this problem requires interrogation of the changing character of the working class, the balance between private and public sector workers in the federation, the social demographics referred to above, as well as 'sins of incumbency' that include business unionism, privileges and commercial opportunities that accrue to shop-stewards (let alone senior leaders), and blatant thievery. But this is not sufficient to explain the impasse that has resulted in the expulsion of the National Union of Metalworkers (Numsa), rending the federation virtually down the middle. Even the ideological differences have always been there, and were in fact more acute during the first fifteen years of democracy. In other words, beyond the objective circumstances are issues of leadership quality across the Tripartite Alliance, including declining legitimacy among the political leaders, occasioned among others by corruption and patronage. All this fuels an irrational and suicidal factionalism.

In other words, the environmental conditions (e.g. slow economic growth, limited fiscal space, changing social demographics and the electricity supply crunch) and the subjective factors (e.g. leadership conduct) do conspire to fuel a sense of crisis in society.

In Lieu of a Conclusion

Theorisation of the South African renaissance ideal should encompass all the elements – both objective and subjective. It should interrogate the detail of technical 'delivery', but do so in a manner that identifies interlinkages and macro-trends and can thus help in conceptualising the long-term trajectory of the changes society is striving to implement. Historically, the profundity of South Africa's (and indeed Africa's) contribution to the social sciences, globally, lay in this sharpness of analysis. Currently, weaknesses in research and teaching in the Humanities and Social Sciences seem to hamper possibilities for creative intellectual interventions that contribute to the realisation of the South African renaissance ideal.

In this regard, to quote a few examples, creative conceptual interventions such as references to a decent standard of living, measures to reduce the cost of living for the poor and how to address spatial manifestations of social exclusion – as articulated in the National Development Plan – do start to raise issues that should engage the minds of South Africa's intellectuals and policymakers. The same applies to discourse on the efficacy of employee share-ownership schemes, profit sharing, and worker representation in enterprises' decision-making structures, as part of the panoply of measures to address inequality. One can add to these the challenges relating to the tension between traditional governance systems in rural areas and the rights embodied in the Constitution. There is also the question whether social compacting can succeed under conditions of weak political legitimacy. At a more generic level there is the fundamental question of whether South Africa is seeking to build a 'nonracial capitalism' and whether this is possible at all! Further, with sub-Saharan Africa showing signs of sustainable growth and development, how does South Africa reorientate its outlook to benefit from and support these possibilities? Many other instances of this kind can be cited, straddling various macro- and sub-themes, all of which require systematic interrogation in our Humanities and Social Sciences.

If the analysis above regarding processes of de-legitimisation and a sense of crisis in society is close to the mark, what are the corrective impulses that will drive a turnaround? Is it the senior leadership of the 'ruling party' as it better appreciates the dangers of these phenomena, and/or the middle-level cadres driven by idealism, but also by self-interest as electoral prospects diminish? Or will it be other political forces, as negative tendencies within the 'ruling party' congeal and become too stubborn to erase? There is no end to questions that deserve comprehensive interrogation.

Intellectuals have an important role to play in ensuring a turnaround from the current sense of crisis. If the country proves unable, in the medium-term, to choose and pursue the positive development trajectory that beckons, South Africa's intellectual community should accept a large part of the blame. The inverse should also stand as necessarily true!

End Notes

1. Professor Thandika Mkandawire, *Introduction to African Intellectuals: Rethinking Politics, Language, Gender and Development.*
2. *Encyclopaedia Britannica Online,* http://www.britannica.com/EBchecked/topic/ 373305/Meiji-Restoration
3. Dr Francis Fukuyama. 2013. MISTRA Lecture.
4. Ezra Vogel, *Deng Xiaoping and the Transformation of China.*
5. Karl Marx, 'The British Rule in India', the *New York Herald Tribune,* 1853.
6. David Scott. 2004. *Conscripts of Modernity: The Tragedy of Colonial Enlightenment.* Duke University Press, p. 113, Kindle edition.
7. Steve Biko, *I Write What I Like* and Pixley ka Isaka Seme 1906 Columbia University Lecture, 'The Regeneration of Africa'.
8. *The Freedom Charter,* adopted at the Congress of the People, Kliptown, 1955.
9. Report of Study Commission on US policy toward southern Africa, *South Africa: Time is Running Out,* 1981.
10. *African Claims in South Africa* (adopted by the ANC in December 1943).
11. Op cit.
12. Nelson Mandela, 'In our Lifetime', *Liberation Journal.*
13. In the document, *The Freedom Charter: Revolutionary Programme of the ANC,* adopted at the 1969 National Consultative Conference, the ANC asserts: 'It is necessary for monopolies which vitally affect the social wellbeing of our people such as the mines, the sugar and wine industry to be transferred to public ownership so that they can be used to uplift the life of all the people.'
14. Report on the Strategy and Tactics of the African National Congress, 26 April 1969.
15. *Ready to Govern,* ANC policy guidelines for a democratic South Africa adopted at the National (Policy) Conference, 28–31 May 1992, as mandated by the 48th National Conference in 1991.
16. George Devenish, 'SA's Constitution provides for transformation and not a radical revolution', *BDLive,* 27 January 2015.
17. For a detailed analysis of the 2014 electoral trends see 'Voting trends twenty years into democracy'. Available at: www.mistra.org.za .

Response – Ben Turok

I think we should start by paying tribute to Joel Netshitenzhe because Joel has been an outstanding intellectual in South Africa over a long time: in struggle, in government, and now outside government. It's much easier for me to engage with him now than when he was in government, although we did engage then. So a tribute to him.

Also, I want to say I agree with a great deal of what he had to say and I wish I had more time to spell that out. I was going to read from his paper the very last sentence: 'If the country proves unable to choose and pursue the positive development trajectory that beckons, South Africa's intellectual community should accept a large part of the blame.' That the intellectual community, namely us, should accept a large part of the blame. I think that is absolutely appropriate and I hope that this gathering ends up by accepting a certain degree of blame and saying what we are going to do about it. You see, I'm with Ibbo: we must do something about it.

I want to then quote a Marxist who was a Russian, not a European, G. V. Plekhanov, 'The Role of the Individual in History', in the volume *Fundamental Problems in Marxism*, and I'm going to quote a paragraph because the role of the individual in history applies not only to leaders but also to intellectuals. So let's hear what he has to say.

> *By virtue of the particular traits of their character individuals can influence the fate of society. Sometimes this influence is considerable, but the possibility of exercising this influence and its extent are determined by the form of organisation of society, by the relations of forces within it. The character of an individual is a factor in the social development where, when, and to the extent that social relations permit it to be such.*

So individual intellectuals, whether they are polemicists or whether they are problematisers or whatever, do have a role – and an important role – but there are limits because they operate within social forces in society that actually constrain the degree of influence they have.

He also says, 'No great man' – and that's great intellectuals – 'can foist on society relations which no longer conform to the state of these forces or which do not conform to them.' So in a sense, we're all captive of the society we live in and, much as we have a role to play – and I think a major role, and Joel has said that we need to lead – that leadership is within a context and we must never forget that context. I certainly believe that the present conjuncture in our country is eminently open for an important role for intellectuals in public discourse to illuminate problems and find solutions.

I also want to refer to a paper that I received last week by Vishnu Padayachee, who made a speech in 2011 at Rhodes University where he dealt with the role of the intellectual in South Africa and the danger of capture by the state. He explains the failure of our intellectuals in South Africa partly by the fact that the government moved to the right and as it did so – we're talking about Gear and related policies – so intellectuals were captured within the state and the movement, which was moving to the right. And I think there's a great deal to be said about that. There's a great deal in his paper that I commend to you. It's a long paper and he does analyse exactly the kind of things we are talking about and tries to explain them in objective, not subjective, terms. It is now common cause, and it has been referred to at this forum, that many intellectuals have retreated into conformism and orthodoxy, while others have withdrawn from public debate.

The next point I want to make is this: the de-legitimation that Joel raised; 'processes of de-legitimation and a sense of crisis in society'. He asked whether there may be corrective impulses to negative tendencies within the ruling party before matters 'catch fire'. He blames weak leadership. I think that's true and I think that there's a general sense in the country that the leadership at many levels is much different to the Mandela era and when Joel was so influential in the Thabo Mbeki period. We do have an intellectual problem in that leadership is lacking and that the intellectuals are not performing the role they're supposed to.

I want to comment on the formulation of Dr Mcebisi Ndletyana. He started off by saying that he's looking at the role of the state, of the intellectual in state formation, suggesting that, in Africa as a whole, intellectuals were preoccupied with playing an intermediary role in the independence and post-independence periods as participants in state formation. It's not entirely true. Many intellectuals were not part of that process, nor were we part of a pure African nationalist history directed at state formation.

Some of us were interested by Marxism and socialism, by international revolutionary movements which went beyond African nationalism, and post-independence politics. There was a current throughout Africa, which was led by people in the Marxist tradition, and they were following not just European Marxists, they were following Mao Tse-tung and Le Duan of Vietnam.

So you see, we cannot portray the Marxist tradition as a purely European phenomenon. It was, I agree with Ibbo, an international phenomenon that was taken on board by Mao in China, by Vietnam and many other forces, not to forget Cuba and our own Kwame Nkrumah. So we shouldn't portray the intellectual legacy of the emergent industrial capitalism in Europe and the theories that arose out of that as a European and, in a sense, undesirable phenomenon. We need to go beyond the notion that African intellectuals were captured within the liberation movements without any additional dimension. Certainly in South Africa, within the ANC, there was the Communist Party and the Marxist tradition, which of course influenced the ANC in many ways without of course capturing the ANC and changing the ANC into a different kind of movement.

To return to the themes raised by both Ibbo Mandaza and Professor Vil-Nkomo, that intellectuals in South Africa do have to rise to the challenge of our current crisis, and I think I'm very happy to hear that people are acknowledging quite openly in this forum that there is a crisis, including a crisis of weak leadership and a crisis of uncertainty, and we must use every tool in the book, wherever they come from, in order to try and find alternatives.

Above all – and I agree with Ibbo Mandaza – that above all the challenge is an economic one. We have lost direction on economic policy. I think the NDP is a very weak document on the economy. It's a good document in many senses, but the chapter on the economy is extremely weak and it seems to me that intellectuals ought to seize the moment and develop alternatives. I would hope that this meeting can begin to do something about it. I refer in particular to the conservatism and orthodoxy that is now hegemonic in government and much of the country that insists that financial austerity is essential and that we must conform totally to the dictates of the rating agencies and foreign investors. I find it strange that we should choose to impose harsh medicine that will stall the economy further when there is a new tendency in the developed countries against austerity and for stimulus, even arguing that inequality is bad for growth.

Let me conclude by a little bit of a commercial. I was irritated by Peter Bruce in *Business Day* writing repeated columns attacking Rob Davies and Ebrahim Patel, and in particular a column about four weeks ago attacking Patel, saying he's a nice man but he's totally wrong and his policies are absurd. So I have asked two very distinguished economists to write a response in the next issue of *New Agenda* on the question of state intervention, private enterprise or both. I think that that question is something that we should all take up to try and develop an alternative to the rubbish being presented to us as national policy in *Business Day* and other business fora.

References

Padyachee, Vishnu. 2011. 'Ideas and Power: Academic Economists and the Making of Economic Policy', Dr A. B. Xuma Memorial Lecture, Rhodes University.
Plekhanov, G. V. 1969. *Fundamental Problems in Marxism*. London: Lawrence and Wishart.

Discussion

Oscar van Heerden:

Just three things: two from the previous input and one for Joel. I disagree with Xolela about intellectuals not being radical. I think intellectuals are people who see through the fog of Christianity and the opium nature of that enterprise; the fog of capitalism and the exploitative nature of that. They are people who, through entertaining ideas and being excited with ideas and through problematising, see through the fog and, if the end result is something better, then you need to find ideas with the aim of negating those things that you think are wrong, and so, hence the radical component that comes into the equation.

My second point is that I understand the argument around the conceptual imprisonment, but I do agree with Ayanda to an extent that, just because the origin of universal concepts which have universal application come from the North, does not necessarily mean that we can't actually use them as tools to problematise and critique. In fact, what we should do as intellectuals is to take those, not reinvent the wheel, but take those concepts and interrogate them and see whether they have applicability within our context. So I'm sure you're not suggesting that because the light bulb didn't come from here we should be sitting in the dark.

My last point is to Joel. I agree with Joel in terms of the last sentence: we must take some blame, but I think far too often we're not talking about the reality of politics of retribution, which is a very key reality in the South African context. Xolela has the guts to do what he does and say what he does. Lots of us don't necessarily have that luxury because, when you look at the politics of retribution that is becoming commonplace, if you don't agree you are dealt with. We see it in Cosatu in terms of the expulsion of Irvin Jim and his cohorts. We see it in the Communist Party with Jara, Langa Zita and many others, whether we agree with them or not. We see it in the ANC, the so-called Mbeki-ites post-2007, as well as Malema and many others. If you don't toe the line, if you criticise, you will be dealt with.

So I just want you to comment on the politics of retribution because the threat is real. The NEC of the ruling party – the entire NEC are employees; not one of the members of the NEC is not employed by government – and so the president of the ANC, who is also the president of the country, has employees when the NEC meets, and we need to talk about that because if you raise your voice, you will be fired, you will be reshuffled.

Brian Dixon:
I'm a gold miner, so I am not particularly well schooled in the highbrow language of the social sciences, but I have an idea. I think one of the important things is to move away from the definition of intellectuals firstly, and start crafting what is the value proposition of intellectuals. I've crafted the intellectual as a thinker and a catalyst. That thinker and catalyst is in a landscape and plays in a certain context with challenges and must be mindful of the experiences that people are having and then needs to go through a pathway from thinking to doing, and I get the feeling that we are a little bit stuck in the thinking space.

But now that pathway is made up of a couple of things. Firstly, we ask questions and we have arguments and that starts clarifying the issues and unpacking them. From that we then have ideas and those ideas start surfacing. We then need to go through a process of demystifying and translating those ideas so that people can make sense of them and that's where the discourse happens and it enhances the ideas and makes them even better, and from that flows innovations and solutions and that collectively drives two things: changing paradigms about the way people think, and changing practices, which means new ways of doing things.

Moss Ngoasheng:
I really find the conversation about intellectuals quite limited in the sense that it's only focused on people who deal with ideas and constructions of words and things. There is a whole range of people who solve problems, practically invent things that deal with social issues that impact on people who never attend gatherings of this nature: people who do innovations about how to improve yields on a farm; how to improve yields in a production process. They never attend meetings of this nature and I think that, as social scientists, we have tended to appropriate the concept of intellectual to ourselves in exclusion of others.

The second point I want to make is the issue about the state and power and the role of intellectuals in that context. Most of us were trained as intellectuals who critiqued and were outside of the state, and we've been battling to come to terms with the fact that we now are the state.

Stranger Kgamphe:

I'm very disappointed about this meeting today, particularly with the old leadership talking the same old language. When Ibbo mentioned 1988 I thought we will talk about the lessons we have learned from African countries as the last country to be free. If you are too close to the bush it's very complex. It's a complex matter that we cannot handle because we have no experience of handling it, and we are going to have meetings like this for the next ten years: talking about ideas of intellectuals, debating about intellectuals. We have on the table now Agenda 2063 with this questioning of African unification for us as a region to be free. None of the speakers touch on the essential aspect of where we should be going in Africa.

Karima Brown:

I've been listening to all the inputs and I must say that I think we're using 'intellectuals' wrongly. I think we're talking here about a political class rather than intellectuals. I look at people who have been making contributions in the fields of HIV, climate change – they're not in this room. The people who are here are former state mandarins, people who were directors-general, who have developed policy, and I think there's a conflation for me in the inputs with the development of a political class and the role of intellectuals. I don't have a problem with looking at the political class in South Africa because I think a lot of the weakness in state capacity relates to that: our inability to develop a political class; the social mobility issues that go with that; the questions of corruption. The fact that the public sector and the private sector are not able to cohere around what needs to be done has a lot to do with why we have people in the state who think their economic futures are tied to that process and it relates to the point that was raised earlier around the politics of retribution.

Lindy Langa:

My question is about the lack of interest around female intellectuals. When I look at the panel it's dominated by males and, where women are involved, they are programme directors. They say 'thank you' at the end of the show and they respond to the question of gender at the end. So we cannot talk about agency. We cannot talk about subalterns. And we cannot talk about the reconceptualisation of hegemonic discourse without recontextualising and reconceptualising the role of female parties in the context of South African nationalists and nationals.

Xolela Mangcu:

The comments we are making that, just because the light bulb did not come from here we should be in the dark, I know you didn't mean it that way, but it's such a good point. I think that we really have to pay attention to it, and I say this coming from the position of being in a university and teaching sociology and all kinds of things. There is extremely little about African anthologies and epistemologies. But what all our students have been exposed to, and are continuing to be exposed to, are Karl Marx and Max Weber. And I say that, inasmuch as I appreciate the need of what sometimes is called syncretism, we will of course pick from the world what is good and create a new idea.

It is particularly important for us to actually look at whether the problems that Joel is talking about also have to do with the fact that the structural system that we have is based on foundations that are alienated from the way that African people think about the world, think about issues of government and all of that. So it seems to me that, inasmuch as we need to pick from around the world, the fact that 99 per cent of African anthologists and epistemologists are outside of our knowledge systems is a very, very serious intellectual problem, and they indeed have something to do with the problems that we're facing as a country.

Joel Netshitenzhe Responds:

First, about definitions and categories, a few questions were asked in that respect. Firstly, just to warn that we should avoid definitions that would suggest, amongst others, that you can only be an intellectual if you belong to my school of thought, if you are radical or this and the other.

Secondly, have we adequately reflected on the other disciplines in contextualising this workshop? Perhaps not adequately, but in the next session we are going to have a professor in social sciences and another professor in artificial intelligence in the natural sciences, and that discussion should help address these issues.

Gender: there can be no rationalisation which would apologise. We can talk about having tried and so on, but I think we should just apologise.

Lastly, on the issue of retribution: I think the point needs to be acknowledged that intellectuals in South Africa, especially from the Black community, are part of the emergent so-called middle class or middle strata, and indeed they would therefore also evince some of the attributes of that emergent middle strata and one of those is the fear of falling because most of them are first-generation middle class, just climbing up the social ladder, and therefore there will be that fear that if you become too critical you might be marginalised materially.

But I would like to argue that there are intellectuals within the ranks of the broad liberation movement who have been critical about things that are happening within and you'll be surprised at the reception from amongst some of the leadership of the liberation movement to these debates.

As I was saying in the conclusion to my presentation, as in business where profit will impel certain actions, in politics the self-interest is about being re-elected and one of the reasons why many would argue that there is a possibility of a turnaround in South Africa, a possibility of self-correction, is because we have a democratic system which, if the political leadership does not respond adequately to, it will then find itself politically marginalised, and therefore critiques that help people to identify problems and resolve them might not necessarily be accepted by everyone, but I think they are welcomed.

You might have noticed – now talking as one of the members of the NEC who is not employed by government – that some of the critiques of the ANC in the political and organisational reports at conferences are even sharper and more acute than what appears even in the media. Perhaps the question is: why is there no link between that and action after these conferences?

Ben Turok Responds:

I want to follow on that to say that the speech by President Zuma at Mangaung at the last national conference of the ANC opened up such a strong criticism of the ANC itself and the corruption within and received applause from 5,000 delegates. So also to suggest that the concerns raised by people here about the weaknesses are also repeated within the ANC and within parliament itself. It's not as though there is a wall of those of us who are smart and outside and understand some of the problems, and people inside who don't understand. The problem is the articulation of that and I think history is going to sort that out somehow.

But what I really wanted to deal with very quickly is the conflation of practice and theory. You know people are talking as though there is a total iron wall between practice and theory. We do need to make distinctions between practice and theory so when people are engaged in practice that is a very important element and should be respected in the way that people have been crying out. But that's not the same thing as developing theory, and those of us who've been in the movement for quite some time were actually stimulated and brought into the movement not by practice but by the theory.

We were fascinated by *Capital*, for example, documents, books like that, by Van Horn, by Che Guevara who articulated the theory of revolution – of course Mao is the major factor in all this – who articulated the theory. For example, the essay on contradictions by Mao Tse-tung, a brilliant essay which I read again and again because it's a theoretical explanation of how contradictions develop within society and within ideas. That's an intellectual exercise. I don't apologise for liking Mao Tse-tung who was the leader of the Chinese Revolution.

So there is a thing called revolutionary theory which is so important, and Lenin and many others have talked about the importance of developing a revolutionary theory in a country, which is different to the practice, although, as people have pointed out, they meet in practice, namely in the organic intellectual who uses the theory to engage in practice.

So I think we've really got to get this thing right: that practice is practice; theory is theory. The important thing is how the two relate to each other: how the one feeds into the other and feeds back. That is the dialectic of human intellectual work and we must understand the distinction and yet analyse the relationship between them. It's so important, and I hope we don't fall into the trap of saying the only thing that's important is practice.

PART THREE

Humanities and Social Sciences in Unravelling the Dynamics of Class, Race and Gender

Humanities and Social Sciences in Unravelling the Dynamics of Class, Race and Gender – Ari Sitas

There have been very few intellectuals who contributed to key ideas that have come to constitute the humanities and the social sciences in the modern world who did so from the lofty towers of the academy.

From Zara Yacob in Ethiopia in the seventeenth century to Rene Descartes in exile in the Netherlands, from Pierre-Joseph Proudhon to Karl Marx, from Jean Paul Sartre to Frantz Fanon, from Walter Benjamin to Kwame Nkrumah, from Ludwig Wittgenstein to Bertrand Russell, people with ideas about the world were outside, or chased out of, universities. I am afraid there is no necessary connection between working in a University and being a real person of ideas. Nevertheless, the universities are absolutely crucial in creating the quality of mind for intellectual work in any country. Universities were, and they will continue to be, spaces that create the conditions for thinking.

As you know, I and Sarah Mosoetsa were tasked with an unenviable task by the Minister of Higher Education to do something about the humanities because there was a perception that we had failed to respond to the challenges facing our society and our continent. So we tried to correct what was deemed 'improper' in the humanities. We developed a Charter for the Humanities and the Social sciences. It was debated, it was celebrated, it was criticised. It felt like everybody was 'at' us. It was 'pie in the sky'. You know, it was – 'oh, if pigs could fly', an eminent academic said, 'nothing will happen of it'. It was an 'electoral ploy' by the Minister, it was 'applied Nationalism' and an 'authoritarian intervention'.

What we attempted to do through the Charter for the Humanities and the Social Sciences was indeed against the grain – we set out to create a post-apartheid higher education system that is honest, critical and courageous and, I hope, Mandela-Gandhi-like in its simplicity.

We needed vision. We asked ourselves: where do visions come from? We have the resources to make it happen. We are not a poor country. We are an unjust one.

We live in a rich socio-economic laboratory, a space that has never been shy of its frontier status. The new frontier would be a search for a humanism in the humanities and for the democratic social in the social sciences on a continent that has been scarred by modernity from the slave trade to the Rwandan genocide. It is about a different jihad and striving that must concern us.

What is needed is an epistemic shift to a postcolonial and post-apartheid knowledge project in the broader social sciences and humanities that is more sensitive to an increasingly multipolar world, and within that a transcription of the main tenets of our fields.

We are in a process of transformation from a deeply regrettable past where the relationship between science and the state and science and society was not an innocent one at all.

Well, it has happened: most of its proposals have been accepted and a National Institute has been created. It has processes and lines of accountability. It has already provided 300 Ph.D. scholarships to Humanities and Social Sciences students. It has generated a whole range of research projects and it is here, working together with the National Research Foundation, trying to do something about the landscape of our learning and teaching.

We erred often, but our first mistake in the higher education system of the 1990s was to start reducing everything to the market. The market became the actual guarantor of scholarship, of education and relevance for a while. Courses, curricula and funding tried to address what a putative market needed, until the process damaged too much and until everybody started trying to correct the damage. By reducing institutional performance to the market, in increasing the flows of goods, people, communications, information and financial transactions, neoliberal initiatives have created a new conjuncture. Shorthand: globalisation.

But all these efforts have not solved the contradictions of 'modernity', they have reconfigured them and exacerbated them. They have not led to a new 'great transformation' but to a dangerous rewiring of the world system and its subsystems. Not only have they increased existential insecurity, they have entrenched processes of exclusion, marginality and inequality that have no moral justification whatsoever. It is a phase where the poor don't matter and the ways people had been clustered have lost their axiomatic grip. Had it not been for the sheer necessity to earn something in money or in kind, societies would have been spun out of control. I will not talk about those implications today and the implications of a crass managerialism that has permeated our institutions of learning.

Today's focus on intellectuals demands that we examine another aspect of the Charter: the necessity of a *cultural* revolution if we're going to achieve anything substantive in the near future. Our charter work concluded that there was never a golden past of the humanities from which they have descended into the 'badness' that we experience today. No, if anything existed that was of value during the apartheid period, it happened despite the system, not because of it. People on the margins of the system generated ideas and they were the exception and not the rule.

The Charter

If you look at the work we've done, you know so far we've identified catalytic projects and I will focus on some of them to illustrate the extent that the cultural revolution is necessary.

There were eleven research areas we started from and there are many more as we speak: of Precolonial and Pre-1652 History; of Turning our World Heritage Sites into Knowledge Centres; of Recovering the Traditions of Popular Education and their Methodological Innovations; of Concept Formation in Indigenous Languages; of the Social Sources of Creativity and Design; of Hidden Voices in Scholarship in Literature, Music and the Arts; of Strengthening HSS Professional Associations; of Strengthening Public Debate and the Intellectual and Creative Life of all Provinces; of Post-Conflict Reconstruction and Reconciliation; of Socio-Economic and Ecological Alternatives; of Afro-Indian and Southern collaborations. Let us explore some of them.

Firstly, we tasked the Mapungubwe Institute to help us think of how to turn our heritage sites into knowledge hubs; how to turn things that turned to fast-buck tourism into knowledge hubs for the preservation and the enhancement of a scholarship that is genuinely southern African.

Secondly, we've instituted a network that tries to create, for the first time, a consensus of what the precolonial history was, what existed between the eleventh and the seventeenth centuries. Was it three polities or twenty? Isn't it sad that we lack such an intellectual work and that the majority's history remains a cypher? So the whole history of this southern part of Africa is an absence, or what exists about it is a bit of archaeological work here and there, or talk about inchoate societies and anthropological objects waiting all of a sudden for 1652 when certain ships arrive around the Cape!

In doing this we are looking for a different narrative:

It starts from who 'we' are – South Africa's story is a story of the southern tip of Africa and it is not about a people discovered by the Portuguese or by the Dutch East India Company. It is a painful story, but no carpet is large enough to sweep it under. In saying this, our task team has often been accused of grandstanding or of 'applied nationalism'. Guilty. We cannot face this with the customary response of an ostrich even if our feathers look good in the wind.

We have recommended, as one of the catalytic projects of the Charter, the turning of our World Heritage Sites into research and educational knowledge centres, not only concerned with biodiversity but concerned also with how to be fascinating Humanities Hubs as well as centres of ongoing research, documentation of know-hows, of oral stories and poetry, of knowledge production, of student internship and education. All these can serve as the kick-start in the process of generating the infra-sources of indigenous and endogenous knowledge systems.

Why should this be uncomfortable? Have we visited the Anthropological Museum of Mexico City? Have we looked at the Smithsonian's collections of indigenous lore, knowledge and social structure? Have we been inside the Cairo Museum? Are we saying that we mustn't even try because the people of this tip of this continent were just an ahistorical, customary mush, a repository of yearning for a bible to be saved through and a ship to be traded in? Were slaves just chattel? Does it matter that they came from Mozambique, Malabar or Madagascar?

This is where we have parted ways, not only with the kind of colonial attitude that insinuates the folly of such a preoccupation, we had to part ways with Frantz Fanon as well when he argued in *Black Skins, White Masks* that 'it would be of the greatest interest to be able to have contact with a Negro literature or architecture of the third century before Christ. I should be very happy to know' ... he argued, 'that a correspondence had flourished between some Negro philosopher and Plato. But I can absolutely not see how this fact would change anything in the lives of the eight-year-old children who labour in the cane fields of Martinique or Guadeloupe'. Or, where a few pages back he asserted that 'the discovery of the existence of a Negro civilization in the fifteenth century confers no patent of humanity on me. Like it or not, the past can in no way guide me in the present moment'.

We would rather have the eight-year-olds in class and not in the cane fields; in proper classrooms learning not only in their mother's tongue but also learning about the traces of a past that will give them existential nourishment.

We have also agreed on a national project to construct, through all available scholarly means, a minimum consensus narrative – an attempted history of broader South Africa from the eleventh to sixteenth centuries as a catalytic project. You are this catalytic project. It is about time that historians, archaeologists, linguists, geneticists and other specialists lay the foundation for all ensuing research and that such research be funded.

It has to build on the work started by the '500 Years' group in Gauteng and the work of scholars in the broader southern African region. That this would involve a hard historical effort of restoration there is no doubt; that there will be gaps and lapses, no doubt – but we do need to be able to say that there were, in the sixteenth century, 10? 11? 12? 15 polities on this landscape and a number of smaller chieftaincies before we can even do comparative historical sociology or anthropology with other regions. Such a reflection cannot occur in isolation of Africa's key interactions with the rest of the world, as Africa has never been a bounded unit throughout its ancient or through its more recent history, and therefore demands a deeply relational understanding of emergence and consolidation.

Thirdly, yes indeed, we are going to interrogate concept formation in African languages: what concepts might help our humanities, and so for scientific endeavour (and that should be developed through all the languages), not to learn isiZulu, but to find the 32 ways through which in isiZulu we speak about poverty, might revolutionise a concept of poverty.

Then fourthly, the social sources of creativity: how is it that the ecology of creativity produces so much talent without the universities, without the schooling systems, and traditions are passed on from generation to generation? Before we mess them up we'd better understand them and understand them deeply.

We have got many other projects on popular education, reconciliation, on reconstruction, and on alternatives, economic and ecological alternatives, and our principle is to network people together and now a new call has gone out for catalytic projects and we hope through that to start generating another subject of the humanities in addition to what existed in the past, devoid of the scars of race, class, gender oppression.

We avoided the grand design but rather focused on specific ideas for specific problems. We avoided fables of success. The university system in South Africa had its own history and it was important to look beyond the European systems to understand how postcolonial societies created vibrant energy points that enhanced their capacity to succeed.

During our deliberations we were very interested to learn, for example, how and why a postcolonial (but an indigenous-repressing and slave-owning society) like the USA was led to establish its Humanities project. Was the Smithsonian Institution an endogenous innovation that came to underpin a successful Humanities and Social Science drive? If, furthermore, one could not just create such an institution *de novo*, what bits needed to be put in place, given our limited resources? What could we learn, as abovementioned, from the Anthropological Museum of Mexico City? From the School of Oriental and African Studies in London? And what could be gleaned from the Chinese Academy of the Social Sciences?

All the above are enhanced by new trading winds – where, of the old so-called advanced capitalist countries, only Germany and Japan remain serious economic partners, whereas the links to China, India, Brazil, the Middle East and the rest of Africa are growing exponentially. We are in the midst of a new wave of industrialisation and a rewiring of the world economy that is located Eastwards and a proliferation of know-hows that are located Northwards and a growth that is orchestrated by the South's emerging powers. What is appropriate? BRICS-like consortia and think tanks? Broader networks than that?

So, furthermore, in collaboration with Codesria and other institutions on the continent, we started thinking bigger. The only way we can have African scholarship is if we create communities of scholarship. We called our joint first tentative step the *African Pathways Programme*, where our students on this continent will move from university to university, will move around and start meeting each other: not South Africa stealing the students from Zimbabwe and Ghana and so on, but us working together to move students around. And there is a whole range of interventions, but they all boil down to trying to create the climate for a new type of intellectual work that's appropriate for a post-apartheid period.

So the quality of mind we're looking for, in other words, is not about the pragmatic adjustment just to the needs of the day, or to corporate needs of clogging a new generation into functions. We might need them to be unclogging themselves out of the present functions to develop the quality of mind that will make them into leaders, problem solvers, and intellectuals. So that's what's happening systemically, and the university system is accepting it, fighting it, and it's all there in an uneasy relationship with it, but it has happened and it's up to you basically if it succeeds or not.

Of Ideas

Whereas the above are systemic attempts to create the context for intellectual work, there are obviously new challenging ideas all around us. Furthermore, I have three things to say at a conceptual level. The first one is that we have to rid ourselves of the idea of progress that makes us believe that all countries are running in an Olympic sprint: you know, like Bolt in this lane, Sitas in that lane, and Netshitenzhe in that lane, and we are differentially kind of endowed and therefore we need to catch up with the Bolt of all of this. Our pasts and futures have been and are interdependent and relational and this world that we are trying to make sense of and the world that we're trying to transform for the benefit of future generations, you know, has to be understood as something that doesn't have a necessary Eurocentric end. I leave it at that.

Secondly, there is incredible work that has been done by historians now around the Indian Ocean and around the Atlantic Ocean, where it just has challenged totally the idea that Europe was a 'virgin' birth, pulled itself right and tight out of its own bootstraps or out of its own womb to emerge in her plenitude. We are talking about civilisational alternatives and clusters of history that our children and ourselves never learned about. We need to come to terms with understanding that in the eleventh century the world was as connected as it is now, a bit slower, but Indonesia talked to Madagascar, to the Nguni coastland, to the East Coast of Africa, to Zanzibar, through the Arabian Sea to Persia and vice versa; and all the artefacts are there, archaeologists know about them, but we don't know about them at universities.

At the same time, our relationship to nature has taken a beating. We know that. Our Latin-American philosopher friends are saying perhaps the problem is partly created by the monotheistic religions that have created the 'subject-object' distinctions, and that 'us' the subject are the centre of the cosmos and that, in other words, nature is to the benefit of 'us'. It is there for humanity's aggrandisement.

So we need to think in new ways at the universities. We are living through a period when, scientifically, the idea of race has been totally discredited, where you can construct skins in laboratories of whatever kind, zebra-stripes if you want, but racism is escalating as a social force all over the world.

Assuming that such a restoration of systems was possible, the epistemological break will open up two complex vistas: a new naturalism with relational and contrary elements, a Marx *sans* his anthropocentrism, because at least his concept of the human was intimately seen as part of nature, and our livelihoods and labour processes were socio-natural interactions and secondly, an open terrain that had still to be cleared of landmines. We need to combine emergent African thinking landscapes from Diagne, Houtdonji and many others.

If, for a moment, we stopped reading the news from a European angle and tried to fathom how this looks from the mid-point of Doha or the extremities of Beijing, Delhi, Moscow, Johannesburg or Brasilia, it is obvious that the old centres of prestige and hegemony and their mutant offspring are fading and, for reasons that are quite rational, they are defensively fanning out discord. There is a potential Syria in all of us.

It is ironic that the capitalist world economy is being powered up by China, India, Russia, Brazil, and all of them in concert, and with South Africa in tow, are powering up growth rates in Africa that keep the zero and minus growth rates of the old world ticking over.

So I will conclude with this last idea: that in the late nineteenth century Britain managed to put together, through its imperial period, a combination of the centrality of the production, circulation, distribution of material goods and symbolic values. There is a real tension emerging in this reconfiguration or rewiring of the world: in the late nineteenth century, Britain and France managed to combine power and value. The former was the obvious capacity to impose a political hegemony and a world market that prioritised its welfare in competition and in concert with other European powers. But it also managed to couple the prestige and hegemony of its symbolic and material goods. France was always in contention for the aesthetic aspect of the symbolic, but as far as educational and cultural capital, Britain was the brand of prestige and the arch-signifier for mimicry the world over. No other country had managed to do that in the past. Since then, Britain has been in decline. The US tried to take on the mantle through the

Cold War and ride on that idea that it should be the hegemon that combined all those. Yet, such hegemony is disarticulating, it's disassembling. Material goods have moved East and South; symbolic goods remain North. South Africa is caught in between. What are we going to make of this disjuncture in world history?

South Africa is caught in-between: asserting a knowledge project is precisely a refusal to outsource our brain in any direction and an attempt to constitute something different within that liminal space of the two sources of value.

We have taken this challenge seriously because, after three years of hard thinking, we are convinced that our post-apartheid knowledge project, if it is to fly, has to have an African body with Asian and Latin American wings in conversation with epicentres of knowledge in the North. But that is a metaphor. We need to stretch out what we might be meaning.

Conclusions

Right, you know the problem: who's going to fix it? It can't be by law, by decree, it's by us as intellectuals challenging the knowledge project, moving towards a post-apartheid dispensation and just doing away with the foundations that reproduce class, race and gender inequalities in our society.

For many of us in the broader secularist liberation movements, we can say now (and this is a very recent consensus) that our moral foundation, and therefore our humanities, has to be built on a post-racist and post-imperial foundation where we are all 'others' and where the 'other' is not surplus and therefore non-exterminable; that the 'other' is not chattel and therefore non-exploitable and that the other is non-excludable. We owe this to very serious struggles for human autonomy.

Thank you

First Response – Tshilidzi Marwala

Thank you very much. Good afternoon. As I was driving here and pondering on the topic, 'The role of humanities and social sciences to transform the dynamics of race, gender and class', I was wondering why I have been invited. As a mechanical engineer who works in artificial intelligence, it is not obvious why such a person would even want to converse on such complex issues. I thought maybe it was because of the word 'dynamics' and I was thinking about the Coriolis forces. I'm sure, Professor Turok, you still remember the Coriolis forces.

I think the whole concept of intellectualism is too biased towards the humanities. I think they've appropriated it. Are the humanities and social sciences the only mechanisms to solve the contradictions that exist in terms of race, gender and class? What is the role of technology to solve such contradictions? And I think there's a great deal of a role that science and technology can actually be able to play.

Why is it that we have evolved to think of social sciences and humanities every time we talk about intellectualism? I think there is a reason. I think the reason why we cast intellect in the humanities and social sciences frame is because of the long tradition from colonialism where there was a relation in which we consumed and the colonialists actually produced. And if you look at the history of making universities in Africa by the colonialists, you will realise that very few institutions were made that actually taught us science and technology, and as a result, much of our intellectualism actually is more in the social sciences and humanities. I think we need to deal with that.

As I was reflecting on the issue of intellectuals I went to look at Wikipedia. I know we might have differences as to whether Wikipedia is a source that we should rely on, but it says, 'An intellectual is a person who engages in critical study, thought and reflection about the reality of society.'

Again, this term 'intellectual', to me, invokes other concepts such as cognitive intelligence, logic, rationality and so on and so forth. It basically means the function of intellectuals is to use their cognitive infrastructure to basically solve problems that actually exist in our society. Of course, in the field of artificial intelligence, we believe that some of these high-level skills are going to be replaced by machines sometime in the future: these skills of analysing are going to be done by machines.

One of my students was trying to develop a translation between Venda and English. Basically, you speak in Venda and then the machine translates into English, and one of the challenges that we faced was that, in Venda there are nine ways of saying 'you': *iwe, inwi, ene, lwone, vhone, lone, tshone* and so on and so forth. So you can see that science, technology and humanities are actually unified and I think it is quite dangerous for us to favour one over another.

Nobel laureate Herbert Simon came up with the concept called 'bounded rationality' which says that a human being will never be able to analyse any material perfectly because he does not have the perfect brain and he does not have all the information. So intellectuals are rationally bounded and what they say is fundamentally deformed.

Moss Ngoasheng has stolen my thunder by saying that there are a great deal of intellectuals who are transforming society in much more meaningful ways, which we do not know about. I looked at the foreign policy report on who are the leading intellectuals. Out of the top ten leading intellectuals, almost half of them were journalists and there were only two scientists: Richard Dawkins and Jared Diamond. I think part of the reason why the humanities and social sciences have appropriated this term is because they have the monopoly over the media and their disciplines have closer proximity to the public media than science and technology. If we just think about science journalism, it probably does not exist in our continent and I think that needs to change.

As I was reflecting on this topic I wondered – between Noam Chomsky and Tim Berners-Lee – who has transformed society the most? I am sure you don't know who Tim Berners-Lee is, but he is the person who discovered the Internet. You can imagine how much social, political and economic transformation has happened as a result of the discovery of the Internet. From somebody sitting in a lab and basically formulating the Worldwide Web, including deciding that it is going to be called 'the Worldwide Web', great transformation happens.

There is a philosophical theory called utilitarianism and I think we need to use this philosophy to establish the degree to which an individual is an intellectual. Utilitarianism basically evaluates objects by their usefulness, so if we take the utilitarian view of how to define intellectuals, I will say that those whom I will deem as intellectuals are those people who have the greatest capability to transform the largest number of people for the better.

Now how do we transform people for the better? I think, in my view, we transform people for the better by maximising the total good that exists on our planet and minimising the total bad that is happening on our planet.

Maybe, in conclusion, I would like to talk a little bit about China. In the twelfth congress of the Chinese Communist Party that was held in 1982, Deng Xiaoping proposed that China must basically tilt intellectuals away from the social sciences towards technology and engineering. As a result, for those of you who have studied the leadership of China, it's basically made up of engineers, and part of the reason why they wanted to do that was because they realised that, in order to transform society, their society, they had to make sure that there are enough productive forces to produce so that they can deal with issues of poverty. Poverty is the root cause of gender inequality, of racism, and many ills in society. The consequence of this resolution on China is substantial.

Recently I read a book that was written by Xi Jinping, the current president of China, and I quote what he says in one of his chapters: 'The third industrial revolution would be a robot revolution: big data, cloud computing, 3D printing.' Now if this is the revolution that is going to transform the twenty-first century, can we afford to just balkanise intellectualism to the social sciences and humanities? I don't think we can.

Thank you very much.

Second Response – Nomboniso Gasa

Mcebisi has desperately tried to neutralise me on this issue and, to some extent, he has succeeded; to some extent he hasn't. I just want to make it very clear that if Barry had told me who was going to be on this panel I would have refused to be here, and I made a mistake of agreeing to a conversation without actually asking who else is going to be there, and this is for the simple reason that I no longer participate in panels where I'm the only woman. So if you can't have other women, I don't want to be part of it.

Secondly, I am 48, 49 now, going on 49. I'm rather tired. I'm tired of my own voice. I'm tired of saying the same things. There is actually a whole range of young feminist scholars who I believe have much better things to say and much fresher ideas than I do. So next time I shall give you a whole list of those people and I would love to learn from them.

Actually, I'm saying this thing very seriously because I do think that I look around and you know, Joel is interesting, but I'm tired of listening to Joel. I want to hear people who come after Joel.

Now I'm told I've got five minutes, so I suppose I've taken half of it. The role of intellectuals in society in terms of gender – I'm not going to talk about gender. This is the other thing that happens when you invite aunties: they come and say their own thing. So I will talk about feminist critical theory, feminist thinking and feminist epistemology, because actually gender is but one part of that. I would have taken a quibble with race and gender and leaving everything else, but the younger ones will deal with you.

So I'm going to structure my presentation in three sections and I'll be very quick. In doing this I'm going to ground it with concrete examples, using individuals, historical periods and key issues, and key questions of the day.

I would like to encourage those who are interested in feminist theory – and particularly how historiography writes about feminism and how we reproduce forms of knowledge around feminism, the feminists and the kind of thinking feminists' thought that we affirm – to read Adrienne Rich's book,

On Lies, Secrets and Silences, because I believe that that book actually says a lot about that which is rendered invisible, even in the limited work that is being done in writing about feminists. One of the issues that she writes about, which resonates quite a lot with many of us, is she looks at somebody like Mary Wosencroft. She looks at how she, in the writing around her and about her and her era, is actually completely dislocated from what happened, so you don't see any other women. It is as if she was the only woman of that particular period and so it distorts the view of her era and the era that went before her, and sometimes even the critical issues that they raise, because often it's as if it was only about the Suffrage Movement, and the suffragettes are actually disconnected from other critical issues that were happening in society, as we are doing today in talking about race and gender as if the women wore girdles and women were still continuing to wear girdles, as if they are not connected to the whole notion of the structural reproduction of forms, not only of knowledge, but forms of being.

So I look at my younger sisters wearing so high, high heels, gravity-defying high heels, and I look at them and they look gorgeous, but then I think about it. I wonder if I would be able to, and I think: 'Oh no – Chinese foot-binding.'

So it's very important that we actually understand how even these forms of being, these forms of beauty, these forms of aesthetics affirm or disaffirm the structural construction of society. That is what feminist theory, and critical feminist theory in particular, teaches us. We think that class is about the factory, but we don't look at what happens when women in the mines go in the shaft with men and men rub themselves up against them. You find all these forms of sexual violence and sexual harassment that go beyond what we are willing to talk about when we talk about the people who belong in the same strata and the people who belong in the same social class. Just go underground at Lonmin and meet the women there and look at the issues: from overalls, the design of the uniform, the physiological issues, because the mine underground is not meant for the female body.

So there are a whole range of complications, and unless we actually engage critically with feminist theory and feminist epistemology, ways of understanding things, we are not going to be able to understand how best we can do this thing. How can we design a lift in such a way that, if I don't want your body to touch mine, it won't? Because as the environment is changing, as technology is developing – particularly if we talk about those contradictions from a feminist critical theory point of view and feminist philosophical point of view – then we begin to understand that even progress, what we see as progress, has got other ramifications in other ways.

Joel is completely shell-shocked by this and has decided that he's never ever going to invite me again because I come and say this – but it is the truth. Men masturbate in their minds by rubbing themselves against women's bodies and women have absolutely nowhere to escape, and we celebrate the fact that women are working in the mines and then we don't want to deal with those kinds of ramifications and difficulties.

Well, a lot has been written about Virginia Woolf and how she says: 'I urge you all to write, and write as if your life depends on it,' and of course, even with Virginia Woolf and writing and so on, one thing that the sister forgot was that some women didn't have a shelter over their heads, let alone having a room of one's own in which they could write. So if you engage critically, Virginia Woolf is coming from a particular class in English society, the British society, then you would actually understand the way in which her vision was informed by her location and her understanding and her place in British society.

Now the earlier period, of course, of the emergence of feminism and feminist philosophy affects all of us in different ways. It affects how feminism itself got introduced, or got validated as a philosophical question in our societies. At a different level, in a different conversation, I would actually have a much longer conversation about how feminism as a thought, as a philosophy, actually predates colonial introduction and conquest in Africa. But that's for another day.

However, feminism in terms of official feminist theory and thought, as we have come to understand it, affirms certain forms of behaviour and this is how it happens in South Africa. So you read people like Cheryl Walker. You read a whole range of historians and people in humanities who actually wrote about the political struggle in South Africa, and they talk about 'womenism', 'motherism', because these women were not, in 1955, exactly feminist, you know, as we understand feminism. If you fight – apparently according to official feminist thought – to save your home and to be with your husband and you don't want to have a pass, apparently that is 'motherism'. That doesn't fall within feminism, and this is a question that we continue to ask actually, as a Black woman who stands here, who thinks of herself as heterosexual, I'm not sure, but that's how I live my life. It becomes very difficult in terms of where do I divide my body: which part of me is Black, which part of me is female, which part of me is short, which part of me is tall, and this is part of what the feminist philosophy and the feminist thought has filtered into our society, where, as a Black woman, if you choose to go into the political struggle in defence of your dignity and that of your children, others will come and say but that's not feminism now, that's actually national liberation, as if there's a Berlin wall between all these things.

So what I'm suggesting is that the way in which feminists have written and thought in South Africa about the feminist project is actually very problematic. It is very Western orientated, but not just Northern and Western orientated, it's also orientated in terms of a particular scholarship even in those regions, and it's very important to actually start unravelling and continuing to problematise this.

As Bell Hooks says, for her the whole issue around equality with Black men is a bit of a problem because actually what she's more interested in is a society where she can be equal with everybody, because if it means being equal and living in misery then that's not the choice for her. So Black men can have that, if that's what they want, and I think what she's saying is that, unless you have a feminist thought and philosophy that actually problematises everything, that throws out everything, unless you are able as middle class to be disturbed when people say a bravo man is walking down the street and as a feminist you are not able to sit comfortably with that, the likelihood that you are also going to reproduce the phantom Black man who's dangerous, it becomes very difficult to actually see how you are going to change society.

So it is about the construction of the very race discourse that we're talking about and the multiple ways in which we reproduce that in our own lives.

Finally, what would I consider to be the critical issues right now confronting feminist intellectuals and a feminist intellectual project? I would want, for example, to actually have a conversation about the meanings, the multiple meanings, of land and land dispossession and the new ways of dispossession that are taking place in our society and how a feminist philosophical project would address that.

Firstly, how it understands it. What do I mean by this? I mean that, in our need to affirm what we think is tradition, African tradition – as if there's one tradition, but nevertheless – we are not consciously questioning the way in which the structure of property and giving property to people is defined along gender lines. In the society which has this Constitution we continue to have issues around inheritance and male progenation, and if you want to ask amongst the progressive intellectual class, both men and women, you'd find that when it comes to that we get conflicted. These are issues I believe that we need to unravel. These are issues that need to sit uncomfortably with us.

The second issue also is around this notion of 'willing buyer/willing seller', which is not even in the Constitution anyway. If we look at how the notion of a buyer and the notion of a seller are understood in terms of policy interpretation, you find a deeply masculinist logic that runs through it, because we continue to believe that property, that wealth (even though some women may be earning a lot and may be keeping their families), that the survival of the family has got to be continued through the male line of identity. And it's not just Africans, Jewish people do the same. Until we try and figure out how our conversations on intellectuals, the role of intellectuals, can put feminism in the centre of the debate (not on the periphery where we call it at the end and say can we talk about gender), but we actually say what would happen if you came into the class question and came into it through a feminist theory point of view.

What would happen if you actually ignored Karl Marx and looked at the women that Karl Marx had sexual intercourse with and whom we know as having been his partners or having been his sexual partners, and actually ask what were they having conversations about? Why is it that Rosa Luxemburg is the only woman in that particular period that we get to know about? What happened to other women? Were they only there for pleasure? Were they only there as uncritical beings? I think not, but I think that we will arrive at these questions, depending on how uncomfortable we want to sit with the questions that confront us.

Thank you.

Discussion

Xolela Mangcu:

I think that what runs through all of the presentations is this need for conceptual rethinking of the concepts that we've inherited, that whether it's Ari's voice or around these questions of conceptual reconfiguration. What I would be interested in is what was the feminism that existed in the precolonial era called? Because, as part of this conceptual challenge that I'm launching against these concepts, it would seem to me that it might be an interesting thing to actually say that that is actually a heritage that we have. Now we're not going to call it feminism or feminist theory, but we are going to call it what it was called in the precolonial era.

The parallel here between the notion of the nation, for example, and the concept *isizwe*, and one of the things that has come up in my work on this most noble issue is that, when you actually start thinking about the notion of the nation, and we think about it in terms of *isizwe* and how people like Mqhayi and Soga were writing about it, it gives you a completely new understanding of the sociology behind the nation and it seems to me those are the kinds of new areas we need to explore.

And finally, the distinction between science and the humanities, because the intellectual has got nothing to do with disciplines. The intellectual, at least in the scholarship, is the idea of not only thinking critically about things, but being public about it. That's why Robert Oppenheimer, the guy who came up with the atomic bomb, is regarded as one of the great intellectuals, because he took his thought and ventured into the public domain, and that's what defines an intellectual.

Lebohang Liepollo Pheko:

My response is going to be kind of a blurb of everything that I've been hearing the whole morning. In terms of the hegemony of knowledge and power: I haven't heard much about the conflation between knowledge and privilege and the fact that there is a strong alignment between male privilege, race privilege, white privilege, and the ability for voices to carry. It is not so much always a case that somebody is cleverer or has better ideas, but that they have the capacity, the resources, the wherewithal for their ideas to carry further across times, across continents, throughout history and herstories, and we see this in the media. It's not as though the best ideas are those that we see promoted, but it's the ones that are the loudest. So, is neoliberalism the best idea because it is the loudest? Not necessarily.

I also have a strong concern with the notion that intellectualism in and of itself can be self-appointed and can also be narrowly defined by the same self-appointed few, and I think that we run the danger of presuming that there are not multiple knowledge systems and critical pathways to solutions.

Finally, I think that in doing so we run the risk of dispossessing ourselves in the African reality by allowing ourselves to be defined, often exogenously and externally, and we become innocent, or not so innocent, bystanders in our own definition of what is nation, what is nationality, what is identity and what is the being of African realities and African epistemic endeavour.

Stranger Kgamphe:

I'm curious to understand this creation of the new humanities and I think it was too easy to accept the fact that we are in crisis in South Africa. I don't think we are in crisis in South Africa. I think Ibbo sold it too quickly. We have a dynamic situation where I think democracy is in action. The complexity is what we have to manage, because if we have reached a point of no return, if we are having a meltdown in terms of societal structures, can we talk about the social cohesion index? If so, we must add the positive things: in South Africa there's no upheaval; there are no bombs exploding around here; there's a sense of stability.

We must also compliment the forces, because I strongly believe that for Africans to practise leadership they must be given an opportunity, and we have a beautiful twenty-year experience in South Africa and we shouldn't be too quick to accept that we are in crisis.

Catherine Kannemeyer:

I'm torn about what to say here because of the level at which we've articulated as intellectuals, supposedly informing people who've had their agency removed and that was a product of an economy, a society, or however you want to characterise it. And that disturbs me because there were questions that Joel asked about the problematic youth. I mean those were not the words that he used. I think that the dimension of technology, how it's changed how people relate socially, the threat it contemporarily presents because of communication, and how we shape intellectualism from a grassroots level or within academic forums are questions which we haven't really wrestled with. I think that the provocation that I want to put out there is that context really matters, and to hear something articulated in terms of utilitarianism, which is greatly problematic, I think would be interpreted as such for a large component of this audience, where context of gender or of race or of poverty weaves such a complex interweb is really dangerous, and the thing that I want to leave you with is that we've allowed people to witness as a result of technology. We have not capacitated them to participate or represent themselves, and this forum reflects that.

Hassan Lorgat:

One of the speakers here earlier said that we don't have a crisis and that we're not killing each other. In fact, people are dying every day. They're dying for opposing illegal tenders. The chief who opposes mining in Hlobane gets killed. They get replaced by a new chief who is supportive of what they want. People die every day.

I was in a workshop with a number of community people and they said that it looks like in KZN every councillor has his hit man, and they've got lists of people being killed for opposing some of the actions. So I really want to ask why is it that the intellectuals don't speak about the people who are dying? Those who differ get killed. Those are the true intellectuals there.

My point I really wanted to raise is that there was a lot of new intellectual knowledge around the workers, around workers' culture, things that didn't depend on formal institutions. Okay, you were academics who worked with them, and it seems that the current regime, the current phase of making intellectuals seems to be too heavily linked to universities. Someone raised issues about people working on climate justice; there are a number of people who didn't know what climate justice issues are but they are working on the impacts of them around this country. So what I'm saying is, maybe the new discourse should try and look outside the universities, then we'll find more creativity.

Isayvani Naicker:

What I really appreciated is that you introduced science and technology to this debate. What we also have to recognise is that the majority of the conversations that occur where I sit on the other side are that science and technology are the predominant narrative, and introducing social sciences and humanities to that, I mean coming from where I come from as a scientist. So it's really nice to have this conversation about grounding in the social sciences and humanities and then introducing science and technology into it.

For me the whole thing is about knowledge, ways of knowing the world, and by introducing science and technology to this debate we need to introduce not just the indigenisation of concepts, as Xolela talked about it, but other knowledge systems. For example, at the Department of Science and Technology we take indigenous knowledge systems quite importantly. How do we relate to those knowledge systems in this conversation in terms of the intellectual resources that we galvanise? They're really important. We've been talking about how we look to the North and the South, but how are we looking to our own systems of knowledge within the South?

Ari Sitas Responds:

Firstly, it's not about who is better and who was more important. If we move away from the idea that the humanities and the social sciences are about greatness or excellence or wonderment or whatever and we take them for what they are, they are the originators of ideas of democracy, fascism. They are the people who perfect torture in terms of psychological experiments.

What we are trying to say is that we have ignored the humanities, and that therefore a quality of mind that is appropriate for us moving into a new space away from the past is being atrophied, and what we are trying to do is work with science and get it done.

My second point is that, indeed, how can we move towards a revolutionary science that revolutionises its technology without war being its subtext? Eighty per cent of the inventions that define our excellence at the moment originated out of landing bombs on people's heads, and are from the Internet too, chemical and biological warfare and so on. The consequences have been used for peace, but what kind of stimuli can we create in a society that is moving hopefully towards peace in the future? What stimuli for a revolutionary science do we need? The minute you talk pragmatics, of course there's more bucks and more things to be made out of science than philosophy. I mean there's no competition there.

The third thing is that, you know, feminism, local knowledge, indigenous knowledge systems and so on, are an absurdity in the university system. You see, it's fantastic; it's happening everywhere. That's where the energy is at the moment. The thing is how to create conditions for its flourishing.

Tshilidzi Marwala Responds:

I do agree, Xolela, that humanities, social sciences and hard sciences are basically one knowledge system. We should not differentiate them. I must also add that I read *Das Capital* while I was doing mechanical engineering in North America and it was actually part of the curriculum. You had to do social sciences if you are in sciences. What we in South Africa have not been able to do is bring more humanities into science and technology, and how do we bring more science and technology into humanities and social sciences?

The reason that is often advocated is that it is expensive because of our university staff to student ratios. In North America, even big universities are actually small. MIT only has 10,000 students, so you can basically tell the student you have to take ten per cent of your courses from other areas and you won't disturb the planning and the calendar of the university, whereas if you do that in South Africa, with the staff to student ratios that we have at a university with 50,000 students, then we basically will be in trouble. I mean that is the reason, but there is a realisation that it is actually beneficial for somebody who is studying theoretical physics to know a little bit about sociology, to know a little bit about economics and so on.

On the issue of utilitarianism, for me it is really an optimisation problem and all these other issues, gender issues, race – those are actually constraints that we need to deal with when we are optimising whatever the objective is that we are trying to optimise. It works, and we have evidence that it actually works.

I think that once we deal with the issue of want, the whole gender problem is actually going to collapse. There is a material aspect of gender discrimination that we need to deal with. There is a material aspect of racism. If you look at the Ku Klux Klan in the United States, you can really see that there is a serious gap in the knowledge of the individuals concerned. Of course we'll always have outliers, but seek ye economic freedom and all else shall follow.

Nomboniso Gasa Responds:

You started right at the point where in fact I have serious problems with Nkrumah: 'Seek ye the political kingdom and all else shall follow.' Very problematic, but can we organise a proper seminar so that we can thrash out this issue because, firstly, if you talk about the level of discrimination, it's very, very different from when you talk at the level of construction of society, the actual foundations of society, and I think that's where we need to go a bit deeper.

I think the issue that you raised, Lebohang, on knowledge and privilege, that's what I was trying to raise. Perhaps I didn't use those words because, when I was talking about Virginia Woolf, for example, I was talking about how one particular individual located in a particular context and privilege and her feminist presence, or her presence in history, almost obscures everybody else who's on the other side.

Xolela, I always get anxious when people want to know what was this called. In feminist scholarship there have been decades of writing about whether it's feminism, whether it's womanism, and African-American women led by Alice Walker came up with the concept of womanism because they wanted to bring the fact that they were Black. So I happen to fall on the side that doesn't agree with Alice Walker because I believe that feminism is about a particular understanding.

Now what was it called in precolonial times? Somewhere in my biog. it says that one of the things that I do is to study the body as a site of struggle through carvings and so on. So how we arrive at this is looking at other forms of knowledge production. If you look at African art and if you look at carvings, if you look at forms of praise poetry, *iziduko* for example, and all those kinds of things, and you look at women's presence and you look at what the early feminists in terms of suffrage were trying to do in asserting themselves and asserting their presence into the record of society, not just voting but into the record of society, you will see that those struggles of women and those struggles of feminist epistemology are in the African continent and actually started much earlier.

So what I would encourage is that we also rely more on how knowledge is produced and wherever knowledge is found. And this is part of the way in which scholarship has evolved – that only if you name it, it exists, and if you can't name it, it doesn't exist. And this is exactly the issue that Adrienne Rich deals with in her book, *On Lies, Secrets and Silences*, because we tend to think that that which we don't see does not exist.

Now in many African cultures and civilisations there are other ways of naming and making present without necessarily using words, and in this perhaps I would refer in particular to the Yoruba cosmology. So I think that, if we want to have a conversation around intellectual conceptual stuff, perhaps we need to open it up. Also open it up to poets, sculptors and other people, especially those who deal with ancient civilisations, and I think it will enrich our conversation.

Lesiba Teffo:

I think the question I had wanted to really pose has been to some extent dealt with, namely epistemic pluralism: to what extent can we succeed in theorising the African renaissance if we ignore indigenous knowledge systems? To what extent can we recreate the state, especially the nation state, if it is not undergirded by indigenous practices, local knowledge, governance, epistemology? I think to some extent it has been dealt with.

But in 1999, there was a conference with exactly the same theme as this one. In the course of preparing my paper for that I came across a paper entitled 'Hang the intellectuals' by Shia Arta, a Nigerian, and I wish, even in the future, that we take that critical view: to what extent have the intellectuals undermined and sabotaged the cause of national revolution and national development post independence?

Jean-Marie Jullienne:

Two things that I would like to mention. One is the discussion between men and women. The word that is described as man, the first word which is translated 'man' is 'anthropos', and 'anthropos' is made up of two words, 'ana' meaning upwards, and 'thropos' is countenance, or opinion of self, and I think, if we accept that word as being the originator and we see that it is an upward countenance of ourselves, there will be no division between us.

The second thing I want to say is that the greatest movement that has changed nations is industrialisation. If we see what Europe went through in the 1600s; if we see what America went through because of the Second World War, and we see what China has gone through with industrialisation, it's a long time for Africa to reframe itself as no longer being a nation or a continent that just digs and ships because that's what was instituted for it, and to see itself as an industrialised power, whatever it needs to get there, whoever it needs to partner with, whatever knowledge system it needs to adopt. It's only when it goes through its industrial revolution that it will be able to do so, and the role of the intellectual will be to bring about that reality. So I very much agree with you. If the robot system is going to be the new system of the world, the new revolution, we must access this revolution in Africa long before the robots come in.

Unknown Speaker:

I made a very interesting observation in just the last session with two fundamentally different ways of thinking, two different thought processes.

One is a very linear engineering and scientific thought process that says: here's a problem, we apply a formula to it, we shoot the pieces out of it and we respond.

Then the other form of thinking was understanding complex systems, which really evolves from the social sciences and the humanities, and that's what they apply, and I think Aristotle is the first guy who started talking about two ways of thinking, and he came up with the linear process, engineering form of thought and the world bought it, and the social sciences and humanities are starting to catch up. It's starting to get a lot more prominence now, but if you look at the whole evolution it's largely been a scientific thought process.

The point is, both are important. But I think we start doing injustice to the complex system way of thinking if we think we can apply linear formulas to multiple parts of the pathway. We've got to ask what is the nature of the challenge that we face? Is it scientific where we can apply algorithms, or is it a complex system challenge? And Rittel from Berkeley spoke about 'wicked problems', and what we're talking about today are really wicked problems. They're not tame.

So the first point is to understand the nature of the problem and what is the appropriate way of thinking to address the problem or the challenge.

The second thing is from the complex systems. I think we have further work to do in terms of codifying complex solutions, developing complex solutions for complex challenges, and I think that's the area of the catch-up that I'm talking about. It's a much bigger challenge.

Unknown Speaker:

I think my good friend Professor Marwala is helping us in terms of understanding science, but I'm afraid he reminds me of the French in 1990 when guys were so excited that they felt that scientific discovery could lead to some people being able to deal with issues of modality, but that's not what I'm hoping to raise today.

I grew up in Nelspruit, and one of the things that some people used to say when the Swazi people were calling for democratic reforms was that a multiparty system was inherently un-Swazi, so I'm very suspicious of calls for Africans to return to the past, because I think what that does is embarrass Africans who seek to critique things that are seen as African. So right now what you see is that what I would call reactionary Africans are very quick to lecture us on African values and when we critique them we are told that we are un-African: we do not understand our African past.

I think that it's important that we look back to our past, but that we should not be embarrassed to critique things that are seen as African. Right now, we are not allowed to say anything about the chieftaincy, for instance. There are views that are being bandied about that really are telling us to return back to our glorious past, and when we say there's nothing glorious about this then we're not African. So I think that that, for me, is a serious issue.

Back in the 50s and 60s there were debates about African philosophy, and there was a sense of embarrassment that we didn't have philosophers, and what needed to happen was that, instead of raising philosophical questions, suddenly political issues graduated in philosophy and political leaders were seen as philosophers when in fact there was nothing philosophical that they were raising. They were political questions.

So I'm very happy with us going back to the past, but I'm saying that, in doing so, we should not allow a situation where that is actually stolen by people who want to defend reactionary practices today.

Tshilidzi Marwala Responds:

Maybe just to correct the misrepresentation: equations are not necessarily linear. You have stochastic, you have chaotic, you have non-linear and so on and so forth, and in fact the issue of complexity is the issue that we deal with quite substantially in artificial intelligence, but I thank you very much for this engagement. I think it is quite useful and I think as a country we are going to benefit from it if we start integrating different types of thinking in dealing with the problems that we face.

Nomboniso Gasa Responds:

Just to thank the last speaker on essentialised notions of Africanity, or Africanism, because I think that's a very important issue and it's part of what we are dealing with and we have to struggle to understand to begin with in the present.

I think it's important to talk about the endogenous. A lot of us talk about indigenous and exogenous, but at some point we need to really come to grips with the nature of the endogenous. The same chieftaincies that we're talking about today, if you look at how their powers have been structured by the state, it mirrors that of the British colonial system and it has to because that is the legacy. So when *ikgosi* sits there on the kraal and says no and this and that, you're kind of like, okay, but that's Queen Victoria, right? But I think what is important is to try and problematise what we think we know about ourselves and our past and what in fact we think we want in terms of the future.

Ari Sitas Responds:

I didn't answer the question about the trade union movement and grassroots intellectuals that were emerging. They were emerging because there was a social movement in a platform that opened up the spaces for people who were predominantly oral, to use anything at their disposal to interpret the world around them, and it was a significant moment. Three things have happened to the trade union movement itself. The way it operates has changed. Secondly, it used to be 75 per cent blue collar, now it is only 50 per cent blue collar. You know, there are 25 per cent with university degrees in the trade union movement at the moment. So its character has changed. And thirdly, there is credentialism that is taking over and therefore education is not about discussing, using your local knowledge system to interpret the world, it's basically to move up that book ladder we've created in order to get more money.

PART FOUR

Some
Additional
Thoughts

Intellectuals, Science, and South Africa's National Democratic Revolution – David Moore and Tshilidzi Marwala

The concept of 'intellectuals', especially 'public' ones, in South Africa and most of the world, has been appropriated by the members of that social category populating the humanities and social sciences. Those in the media following in their footsteps create and perpetuate this misperception. Scientists of the 'harder' variety get short shrift. Surely this lacuna is detrimental both to society at large, in which the benefits and pitfalls of scientific research and technological innovation – and the processes leading to them, which are just as important, at least for those believing democratising science would be a good thing – should not be isolated in laboratories and then released to an unsuspecting public through the mechanisms of the 'market'.

These issues are extremely important in any society, but are especially so when a large proportion of science's advances lead to unprecedented increases in economic productivity – in other words they are labour *saving* – and unemployment is a huge problem.[1] South Africa's modes of production are unevenly articulated; it is thus blighted with huge un- and underemployed reserve armies of labour.[2] Thus, one of the main priorities of those guiding South Africa's national democratic revolution is creating jobs (or the conditions enabling such) worthy of a consistently working proletariat that will take the NDR to its next stage. It would seem imperative, then, to encourage more open scrutiny of a science and technology genus seemingly exacerbating the huge inequalities that arise most glaringly in BRICS[3] but are an integral part of a post-1980s conjuncture wherein the 'plutocrats' are ruling the world once again.[4] Thus, the scientists' de facto, but often closeted, position in the intelligentsia would become public and perhaps 'organic' – to anticipate Gramsci's thoughts for a moment – with the social forces that could take the NDR (or NDS, for those who prefer 'society' instead of 'revolution' and thus a softer form of the once Marxist-Leninist formulation) forward.

There are many reasons for scientists often missing the public intellectuals' boat in South Africa's particular manifestation of the postcolonial phase, in which the dynamics of race, gender and class take on all sorts of special characteristics deriving from a unique, albeit globally contextualised, history. They range from the disparate nature of an education system that was and remains highly skewed against the sciences, by default privileging the disciplines emphasising people's outward behaviour, to the special nature of South Africa's political past. 'Science' was often deployed in the interests of segregationist and apartheid policies (themselves with deep roots in the falsities of eugenics, phrenology and the like, integral to the imperial/industrial project, by chance led by pale people from the North whose 'scientists' in these fields justified their privileges and the darker hued – or even paler if they were Irish – subalterns' subjugation[5]). But better science, combined with more rational ideologies that came about in tandem with that better science, soon demolished them.[6] The *political* response to apartheid, however, was often led by *struggle-ista* intellectuals whose repertoire often privileged party line and propaganda over critical engagement: such are the vicissitudes of the blends of Stalinist historiography (often misnamed 'science') and maintaining an intellectually united front against the likewise blinded citadels of racial-capitalist power. Similarly today, public intellectuals of a critical bent – be they liberals or what the defenders of power call 'ultra-leftists' – focus on politics (and political economy if they dare to be a bit more 'scientific') and feed into the media's propensity for an audience whose reach has been conditioned by decades of promised paradises that deliver dystopias. This history, conjoined with a popular culture seemingly dominated by symbols of instant gratification and entitlement – which when denied, and in the absence of a steeled class force, produce paroxysms of discontent rather than the considered praxis necessary for a comprehensive counter-hegemony – produces more artificial intellectuals than artificial intelligence.

How can scientists gain a place on this rather leaky boat, badly in need of some quick, yet sustainable repairs? Where are the resources in an often discredited – often rightly so – tradition of the 'national democratic revolution' to facilitate such a rescue operation? We will argue that Antonio Gramsci, a Marxist revolutionary – the leader of the Italian Communist Party who spent most of his writing career in Mussolini's prison cells – offers some insights along this road. Gramsci was surely the theorist of intellectuals *par excellence* and he would have agreed with the idea that scientists are intellectuals, and perhaps 'organic' or rooted in one of the fundamental classes, at that. It is necessary to repeat Gramsci's most important injunctions about intellectuals. First: everyone is a philosopher; everybody can be an intellectual; nobody is stupid, but the common sense that clouds our minds can be turned into *good sense* if decent education is available universally. This can only be provided by the 'Modern Prince' (*Prison Notebooks* speaks for the Communist Party) if it gains power and can 'educate the educators': after all, Gramsci was probably a Leninist in the end, at least in the 'East' (Russia circa 1917 but by extension the 'Third World' now) where civil society is 'gelatinous' and democracy is ill-fitting, and therefore a difficult site on which to build a new form of hegemony before the frontal attack on the state, which 'was everything'.[7]

Gramsci was not an elitist such as those who say he was wrong to suggest that anyone can be an intellectual (they tend to preclude scientists too).[8] However, and secondly, only a few organic intellectuals – a select stratum in and of the fundamental classes – have the social, political and economic *function* of intellectuals, being in the position of creating and maintaining the 'moral and intellectual leadership' or hegemony for their class. In his elaboration of the notion of organic intellectuals, Gramsci includes scientists among those who exercise 'an organisational function in the wide sense – whether in the field of production, or in that of culture, or in that of political administration'.[9] Scientists most assuredly play a big role in the world of production, and the fact that Gramsci placed the immediately material before culture and politics indicates that he foregrounded the basics of accumulation and its means, contra many posthumous exhumations of his thought that prioritise society's superstructures. It's pretty hard to argue that automobiles and iPads do not function to cement the power of capital – both by making it more efficient and by emphasising the individuality of their users. It's also difficult to refute the fact that the massive collective effort involved in conceiving, executing and utilising these technological marvels means human beings are involved in social and technological processes far beyond their individuality – thus illustrating one of Marxism's fundamental assertions about the contradictions between the essentially cooperative modes by which we produce and use commodities and the 'alienated' ways in which we perceive them. Scientists are at the centre of that vortex.

Before one waxes too wildly on Gramsci and scientists, however, it should be noted that the word 'organisational' above is key. Gramsci focused on the revolutionising of the 'science' of production in the United States of America, particularly on the assembly lines and consumerism ushered in with what he perceptively called 'Fordism', a mode within what Bob Jessop labels 'regimes of accumulation' that has been paralleled, if not superseded, by lean and just-in-time production.[10] But it is not a big stretch from Gramsci's words on Frederick Taylor's 'scientific management' entailing his fine-tuning of the 'trained gorillas'[11] in the huge factories that underpinned the USA's global power and the scientists who today have us salivating and gobbling fast food until we are satiated – and obese,[12] or the logistics experts who have forged Walmart into a global behemoth but whose un-unionised workers look like they have eaten nothing but the Doritos and Coke created by these manipulators of our desires. Ditto for Google's inventors and the creators of Amazon, Microsoft and Apple: even if the Gates's and Jobs's of the world aren't quite Newtons, Watts's and Einsteins and they stand on the shoulders of Tim Berners-Lee, the much less-known inventor of the Worldwide Web, and the collective (with lots of state intervention) including Leonard Kleinrock, J. C. R. Linklider, Vinton Cerf, Robert Kahn and the many others behind the Internet more generally, they manage to combine their scientific wizardry with a presence in popular culture that verifies modern capitalism's common sense – they are extremely rich, encourage insatiable consumerism to keep up with their reinventions of the Joneses,[13] have their own philanthropies to boot.[14] Moreover, this technology has enabled the rise of ideologies and identities within capitalism that appear to compete with and transcend the old hierarchies of patriarchy and control – the rise of what Priestland calls the 'creatives'[15] and feminism in the 60s followed computerisation and the pill, not to mention the 'science' of sexuality instigated by Alfred Kinsey.

This recent history of the combination of science, technology and political economy has transformed our relations to nature and each other. These revolutions have created the conditions in which the world's wealth has increased exponentially – but combined with the economic 'science' that has helped free capital of the Keynesian regulations that evened things out in the past, have contributed to immeasurable gaps between decadent and destitute, even whilst the lifestyles practised by the world's richest are more visible than ever by the poor. The benefits of science and technology are so close but so far that they appear to be replicable only in parody – mostly unconscious, many times in full theatrical regalia[16] and sometimes in combination with the songs and dances that mock power but never dislodge it.[17]

Thus one must leave Gramsci's considerations on science for now and investigate the effects of its very human endeavours in societies such as South Africa, where the old and the new coexist in as much contestation as the inextricably intertwined rich and poor (an indication of which was evidenced in April 2015 when a 'king' is accused to have induced a wave of xenophobia with his unfortunate utterances[18]), but where 'development' has reached the level of semiperipheral or BRICS status. What is the public role of intellectuals with a scientific bent? One can take a utilitarian stance on such a question: what role can scientists play to transform the largest number of people's lives for the better, within a society marked by the tensions that some theorists think can be resolved by invocations of the 'national democratic revolution' – that is, in societies in which there is not a fully developed bourgeoisie nor working class, so the prospects of plenty within a socialist transformation are projected into the far future? This perspective either allows 'the market' to carry on the task of primary accumulation and capitalist development or, with more than rhetorical adherence to developmental state discourse, encourages strategic state interventions to create the public goods that will hasten the developmental trajectory.[19] What combination of state and market can work to assist science to transform people for the better by maximising the total good in South Africa?

It is ironic that, although scientists do not appear to have the honour of membership in the public intellectuals club (held almost as a monopoly by humanists and those buttressing their status as students of the social by the appendix 'science'), the most imperial of the social studies claims the status of science to itself: all the social disciplines tremble in awe at the parsimonious elegance and law-like certainties of economics, and they are at risk of being absorbed into its assumptions, presumptions and methods.[20] Political economy, premised on the unstable relationship between power and accumulation, escapes this sin unless it is perverted by the comical certainties of dialectical materialism, and in any case it has been long banned to the dark corners of academic respectability, making mild interjections from the interstices of the main disciplines or riding such interdisciplinary pursuits as 'development studies'.

A major drawback in these imperial claims and obsequiousness to them is the fact that social interactions contain many more variables than the laboratories of physics and chemistry, the bodies of biological subjects, the circuitry of motherboards, or the networks of cyberspace: it is impossible to extrapolate the same certainties from them as one can in the hard sciences. Thus the models the kings and queens of economics draw up are limited. When even more variable disciplines such as political 'science' resort to mathematics, the results are even further from the vexed and contradictory realities of power. Yet, the *methods* in both forms of sciences can be similar: ask good questions and carry out careful research and the road to knowledge will proceed, either via the accumulation of evidence and argument gradually changing perceptions and eventually the world, á la Conant, or creating paradigmatic revolutions when the old dies and the new rises from the ashes, á la his student and challenger, Thomas Kuhn.[21]

Much of the development discourse in the past few decades has proceeded from preconceived answers rather than questions. When, in the late 1970s, the old world of Keynesian economics appeared to die, a certainty of biblical proportions emerged to replace it. Neoliberal economics (get rid of the state and the market will get all right) seemed to be the way to nirvana. When, after another decade passed and efforts to create communism out of the unevenly developed social formations of Russia and China came to rest, the liberal democratic dream accompanied its economic soulmate on another quest. In another few years, the gurus of global good governance admitted that the state could not be jettisoned (for one thing, there is no other institution that can force the process of primitive accumulation and the birth of private property), but they started to wonder how to restrain the advocates of democracy from asking for too much and straining the public purse: remember Friedrich Hayek's suspicion that democracy was just a way for the poor to take from the rich.[22]

In the current conjuncture, there are no certainties aside from a constant worry that an ideological void on the peripheries of the global system is being filled by the likes of Boko Haram and various caliphates: in their wake, the hubris of liberal imperialists has been shaken.[23] So too has Hayek's invocation that, since no one institution can judge society's needs, anarchic voluntarism (in other words, the market, minus the monopolies his long dead mentor knew would come into it without regulation) should rule.[24] Joseph Stiglitz and his colleagues realised that markets do not disseminate information symmetrically: states can help distribute this public good (and where markets are not fully developed and the state is far from a neutral economic agent, analysis based on assumptions of perfection are flawed). Hayek's void can also be filled by Herbert Simon's insights about bounded rationality gained from experience in the administrative world rather than Hayek's imaginary repository of freedom: human beings cannot analyse any phenomena accurately because they have neither perfect brains nor perfect information. Thus, neither individuals in capitalist markets *nor* states can plan perfectly! In the middle, Charles Lindblom's bureaucracies muddle through.[25]

It should be clear that the utopias cannot be found in states or markets.[26] Teleologies leading to either often come to a halt in 'emerging markets' such as South Africa. In the absence of certainties in the social sciences and policy practice there are only a few priorities that will hasten the development of citizens' rigorous creativity, and thus the human relations and productive forces that will register 'a better life for all'. One of them is the encouragement of scientific method – open, free of cant, empiricist but critical – across all that engages inquiring minds and through the institutions that should foster them. That requires an overhaul of South Africa's basic and higher education. The first step – taken only haltingly in more than two decades of 'democracy' – is the creation of schools equipped to generate what Belle Bogg, in a study of the appalling lack of such in the country upon which most of the world gazes with jealousy if not respect, calls 'the science of citizenship'.[27] Secondly, universities that have not already done so should seriously consider offering – indeed making them compulsory – real science courses to humanities students and vice versa.

Concurrently, those practising the 'sciences' of economics and policymaking must cooperate so that the technologies of production can get more people working: to do this they must abandon fantasies that trickles from market mechanisms will create jobs and, equally, mantras about 'developmental states' without the means to implement them. Along the way to that path, more funds and the capacity to use them are needed for scientific research (including comparative studies in the political economy of developmental states and the ways technological innovation has been implemented in them). If spending on research and development would go up from the measly 0.76 per cent it was in 2010[28] – the lowest of the BRICS – that might be an indication someone was thinking along these lines. However, for any of these possibilities to come to pass, scientists must take up the cudgels of public intellectualism: humanities scholars can't play the game of hegemonic construction on their own.

End Notes

1. John Lanchester. 2015. 'The Robots Are Coming', *London Review of Books*, 37:5 (5 March), pp. 3–8.
2. Steven Friedman. 2015. *Race, Class and Power: Harold Wolpe and the Radical Critique of Apartheid*, Scottsville: University of KwaZulu-Natal Press; Sarah Ferguson and David McNally, 'Precarious migrants: gender, race and the social reproduction of a global working class', *Socialist Register 2015*, London: Merlin Press, 2014, pp. 1–23; David Moore, 'South Africa's xenophobia of a special type: Comparative and historical perspectives', *Mail and Guardian*, 8–14 May 2015.
3. Brazil, Russia, India, China and South Africa – representative of the 'emerging economies' of countries in the semi-periphery of the global system, formerly of the 'Third World' but now moving beyond that status and with significant relative regional and global geopolitical importance (South Africa's economy is very small compared to the rest but is a giant in terms of African political economy, notwithstanding Nigeria, so its membership is justified).
4. Crystia Freeland. 2013. *The Plutocrats: The Rise of the New Global Super-rich*, London: Penguin; David Priestland. 2013. *Merchant, Soldier, Sage: A New History of Power*, London: Penguin.
5. Anne McClintock. 1995. *Imperial Leather: Race, Gender and Sexuality in the Colonial Conquest*. London: Routledge.
6. Saul Dubow. 1995. *Scientific Racism in Modern South Africa*. Cambridge: Cambridge University Press.
7. Antonio Gramsci. 1971. *Selections from the Prison Notebooks*, Quintin Hoare and Geoffrey Nowell-Smith (Trans. and eds.), New York: International Publishers, p. 238; Sue Golding's *Gramsci's Democratic Theory: Contributions to a Post-liberal Democracy*, Toronto: University of Toronto Press, 1992, charts Gramsci's struggles to break free of vanguardist constrictions, as does Friedman's version of Wolpe in *Race, Class and Power*. See also Dylan Riley, 'Hegemony, democracy, and passive revolution in *Gramsci's Prison Notebooks*, *Californian Italian Studies*, 2:2 (2011), pp. 1–23.
8. As Xolela Mangcu stated at the roundtable from which this chapter emanates.
9. Gramsci, 1971, p. 97, also p. 5. Cf. Richard Seymour, 'Gramsci on Americanism and Fordism', *Lenin's Tomb*, February 27, 2011, accessed April 28, 2015, at http://www.leninology.co.uk/2011/02/gramsci-on-americanism-and-fordism
10. Bob Jessop, *L'economia Integrale, Fordism, and Post-fordism*, Italian-Japanese Conference on Gramsci, Tokyo, 15–16 November 1997. Accessed 15 April 2015 from

http://members.jcom.home.ne.jp/katori/Jessop_on_Gramsci.html

11. Gramsci, 1971, pp. 609–10, reflecting on Taylor's phrase.

12. Michael Moss, 'The Extraordinary Science of Addictive Junk Food', *The New York Times Magazine*, 20 February 2013.

13. Robert Skidelsky and Edward Skidelsky. 2013. *How Much is Enough? Money and the Good Life*, London: Penguin.

14. Freedland. 2013, pp. 70–6, 246, 264, 267.

15. Richard Evans, 'Merchant, soldier, sage: A new history of power by David Priestland – review', *Guardian*, 23 August 2012.

16. Freedland. 2013. *passim*. Sibongile Nkosi, 'Burn after wearing – township kids' hottest fashion statement', *Mail and Guardian*, 28 October 2011.

17. Achille Mbembe. 1991. tr. Janet Roitman, 'The banality of power and the aesthetics of vulgarity in the postcolony', *Public Culture*, 4: 2, pp. 1–30; Mbembe. 2003. tr. Libby Meintjes, 'Necropolitics', *Public Culture*, 15:1, pp. 11–40; Mbembe. 2001. *On the Postcolony*, Berkeley: University of California Press.

18. Matuma Letsoalo, 'King Zwelithini blames "third force" for violence', *Mail and Guardian*, 21 April 2015. For comparisons with Zimbabwe, see David Moore, 'Traditional authorities and the new peasants in ZANU-PF's Zimbabwe', *Custom Contested*, 30 September 2013, http://www.customcontested.co.za/chiefs-and-zanu-pf/

19. David Moore. 2004. 'The second age of the third world: From primitive accumulation to global public goods?' *Third World Quarterly*, February, 25:1, pp. 87–109.

20. Ben Fine and Dimitrous Milonakis. 2009. *From Economics Imperialism to Freakonomics: The Shifting Boundaries Between Economics and Other Social Sciences*, London: Routledge.

21. George Reisch. 2012. 'The paranoid style in American history of science', *Theoria: An International Journal for Theory, History and Foundations of Science*, 27: 3, pp. 323–342.

22. Rita Abrahamsen. 2000. *Disciplining Democracy: Development Discourse and Good Governance in Africa*. London: Zed Books.

23. This section is abstracted from Moore's 'Development discourse as hegemony: Towards an ideological history, 1945–1995', in David Moore and Gerald Schmitz (eds.), *Debating Development Discourse: Institutional and Popular Perspectives*. London: Macmillan, 1995, pp.1–53; '"Sail on, O ship of state:" Neo-liberalism, globalisation and the governance of Africa', *Journal of Peasant Studies*, 27:1 (1999), pp. 61–96; 'The World Bank and the Gramsci effect: Towards a transnational state and global hegemony?' in David Moore (ed.), *The World Bank: Development, Poverty, Hegemony*, Scottsville: University of KwaZulu-Natal Press, 2007, pp. 27–62; 'Conflict and after: Primitive accumulation, hegemonic formation and democratic deepening', *Stability: International Journal of Security and Development*, 4, 1 (April 2015), 1–21; 'The end of liberal history in Africa? The demise of a democratic dream and the (re)rise of authoritarianism', *Socialist Register 2016*, forthcoming.

24. Andrew Gamble. 1996. *Hayek: The Iron Cage of Liberty*. Oxford: Polity Press; Richard Cockett. 1994. *Thinking the Unthinkable: Think-tanks and the Economic Counter-revolution, 1931–1983*, London: Harper Collins.

25. Charles Lindblom. 1959. 'The science of "muddling through"', *Public Administration Review*, 19:2, pp. 79–88.

26. John Gray. 2007. *Black Mass: Apocalyptic Religion and the Death of Utopia*, London: Allen Lane.
27. Belle Bogg. 2013. 'The science of citizenship', *Orion Magazine*. Accessed on 1 May 2015 at https://orionmagazine.org:443/article/the-science-of-citizenship
    Bill Freund. 2012. 'Doctoral studies in South Africa', *Transformation*, 80, pp. 69–75.
28. Tamar Kahn. 2014. 'SA research spend falls for fourth year', *Business Day*, 16 January.

The Role of Intellectuals in the State-Society Nexus –
Z. Pallo Jordan

[I begin with a necessary caveat: The term 'Black' as employed in my writings is not a polite way of saying 'Kaffir', 'Native' or 'Bantu'. It is used in the spirit pioneered by the Black Consciousness Movement to include all those who were racially oppressed under colonialism and apartheid. The term 'African' is used as conventionally understood after the 1930s debate in the African language press.]

A passage written by Olive Schreiner, the pioneer South African socialist and feminist, in her 'Thoughts on South Africa' captured the central historic challenge facing modern South Africa beautifully:

> *Wherever a Dutchman, an Englishman, a Jew and a native are superimposed, there is a common South African condition through which no dividing line can be drawn... South African unity is not the dream of a visionary; it is not even the forecast of a genius, which makes clear and at hand that which only after ages can accomplish...South African unity is a condition the practical necessity for which is daily and hourly forced upon us by the common needs of life; it is the only path open to us. For this unity all great men born in South Africa during the next century will be compelled directly and indirectly to labour; it is this unity which must precede the production of anything great and beautiful by our people as a whole; neither art nor science, nor literature, nor statecraft will flourish among us as long as we remain in our unorganised form. It is the attainment of this unity*

which constitutes the problem of South Africa. How from our political states and our discordant races can a great, a healthy and organised nation be formed?

The historical irony of modern South Africa is having called into being a modern political economy through colonial conquest and rapid industrialisation, the white capitalist classes and their supporters marshalled every political device to evade its socio-political consequences – the emergence of a common society in which whites and Blacks are not merely mutually dependent, but are inextricably intertwined by the centripetal forces generated by capitalist development. The intellectuals in the service of these capitalist classes devised policies that constrained rather than released the energies of both the working class and potential entrepreneurs. Their vision seemed not to extend beyond an economy sufficient to serve the white minority alone.

By the cunning of reason, *progressive intellectuals, located in the national liberation movements and organisations of the Black proletariat* became the most consistent proponents of Olive Schreiner's vision by unequivocally embracing the multicultural, multilingual, multiracial, multi-faith society that is the principal outcome of a century of capitalist development. For a century, successive white governments, ably assisted by the white intellectuals who confected their hare-brained programmes and theories, tried to unscramble that historic omelette. Consequently, a vital dimension of twentieth century South African history was the striving of the progressive intelligentsia, the majority of whom were/are Black, to either realise the full potential of South African capitalist development or to move beyond it in the direction of a post-capitalist society.

The democratic political tradition in South Africa has been sustained and elaborated by the national liberation movement and its allies in the movement of the Black working class. It is that movement that has consistently upheld democratic principles and advocated them despite political repression.

The urgent need to develop a civil service with a non-racial and democratic ethos after the 1994 elections drew large numbers of progressive intellectuals into the civil service and other institutions of the state. The policies and programmes of the democratic government are the product of their intellectual labours.

Thousands of others intellectuals remained outside the state, pursuing careers in academia or other professions. The authorship of the democratic government's policies does not exempt them from critical scrutiny. However, it would be ill-advised to regard all and every criticism as driven by the same motives. While some critics may want to hold the governing party's feet to the fire with the aim of improving its performance, there are others whose purpose is the infliction of third degree burns or other injury to its feet!

It is a well-established fact that democracy created unheard of opportunities for Black intellectuals – not only in the civil service but especially in the universities, the law courts and even in industry.

- The majority of South Africa's universities now have Black vice-chancellors;
- Most of the judges serving in South Africa's judiciary are Black; and
- Black technicians are at long last being recognised in industry.

Would it be unreasonable to expect progressive intellectuals to support the democratic dispensation?

Is it irrational for them to defend the democratic dispensation?

Is it unreasonable that the political movement that has most consistently struggled for democracy might also expect their support?

In an important though underappreciated paper, written back in 1987, the University of the Western Cape sociologist Ivan Evans raised the question: '… who shapes the content of intellectual life in South Africa?'

He answered that question in a manner that raised many eyebrows in the ranks of the movement and those of academia:

> …the racial character of the academic process may itself be part of the system of racial domination. To put the matter bluntly: the fact that whites dominate the academic process should be regarded not merely as an effect, but also as one of the objective mechanisms which sustain racial domination.

Evans was writing in pre-democratic South Africa but his proposition, that whites dominate the intellectual life of South Africa, needs to be weighed in earnest. That contention is thrown into sharper relief precisely because we now live in a democratic South Africa.

Any discussion of the role of intellectuals must unapologetically examine whether Evans's observations in 1987 remain true today. If Evans' conclusions remain valid, the majority of South Africa's intellectuals are drawn from the previously racially privileged sector of our population, which still enjoys advantages arising from the statutorily enforced racial privileges it enjoyed in the past.

But serious study demands that we recognise that, although all the liberation movements – from the ANC down to the most recent pre-1990 formations – were inspired by and given leadership by intellectuals, *as a stratum, Black intellectuals played a highly variegated role during the decades of colonial and apartheid oppression.* Not one homeland government or administration would have functioned without their participation. K. D. Matanzima of the Transkei was a trained solicitor; Ntsanwisi of former Gazankulu was a professor. No separate development institution for Coloureds would have operated without the active participation of elements of the Coloured intelligentsia! Amongst Indians the picture was slightly different because such roles were often assumed by the merchants.

It was the radical section of Black intellectuals who articulated the aspirations and identified with the objectives of the oppressed. The conservative and reactionary element amongst them consisted of the principal collaborators and agents of the oppressive system. The tension in the conduct of this stratum is undergirded by the ambiguities of its societal role.

From day one of our democracy, there have been intellectuals who were unhappy with its outcome. The majority of white intellectuals, aggrieved by the loss of power and racial privilege, became the loudest hecklers and faultfinders of our democratic dispensation. Amongst Black intellectuals, there are those who feel that parliamentary democracy is far too little. Yet other Black intellectuals feel their ethnic claims have been compromised.

The substantive question therefore is: 'The Role of *Progressive* Intellectuals in the State-Society Nexus?' Those who are displeased with and opposed to democracy have clearly defined their role – that of an unelected opposition.

Intellectuals as Critical Voices

The first modern intellectuals amongst Black South Africans were clergymen and teachers. The generation who inspired the formation of the ANC were independent professionals, lawyers and newspaper editors. For the first six decades of the twentieth century that remained the situation, but the teaching profession and the church continued to be the points of entry into the professional strata. The national and working-class movements also produced what Antonio Gramsci would have called its 'organic intellectuals', who owed their training to the movement itself and active participation in national and class struggles.

After the destruction of the landed African petty bourgeoisie, South Africa's Black intellectuals were drawn from the professional strata reproducing itself, or from among upwardly mobile members of the working class and rural poor. Colonialism and apartheid having dispossessed the Black propertied classes, no Black intellectuals come from the capitalist class. The exceptions are the Indians. In addition to the professional strata and the working class, a relatively prosperous merchant class has contributed its quota of Black intellectuals and professionals from the Indian community. The shared experience of Black intellectuals as members of oppressed communities, their existential situation and their class origins, reinforced identification with the cause of the poor.

Twentieth century South African political thought evolved as, and is dominated by, two broad intellectual currents. The first was the colonial white supremacist tradition that morphed into apartheid after WWII. The other was a liberal-democratic/radical tradition of which the radical Black intellectuals, supported by a small minority of whites, became the principal custodians. This second tradition was inspired by Christianity, liberalism and Marxism. Those Black intellectuals who opted for ethnic politics and so-called 'authenticity' sought and tended to find political allies among the white ruling class.[1]

After well-nigh a century of struggle, in which the proponents of this second tradition marshalled every strategy, culminating in a liberation war that entailed mass struggles and international solidarity, an environment that compelled the racist regime to negotiate was created.

The Convention for a Democratic South Africa (Codesa) was essentially a contest between these two major traditions. Only the ANC, the SACP, NIC-TIC, the PAC and affiliated bodies advocated a unitary state at Codesa's first sitting. All the other parties, including Zac de Beer's Democratic Party, supported one or other form of consociationism. Whether as federalism or under some other guise, their purpose was to give the white minority a veto over majority decisions. All these other parties sought some means of thwarting the will of the majority. That segment of progressive intellectuals who regarded themselves as the radical 'left', organised in formations like Azapo and Wosa, refused to participate in Codesa. The PAC, too, withdrew at some point. The IFP, playing a reckless game of brinkmanship, pulled out and first aligned itself with the white far right. At the eleventh hour, the white right having demonstrated its impotence, the IFP decided to participate in the elections. Effectively, the negotiations at Codesa involved the vision espoused by the intellectuals, aligned with the ANC and some of the homeland parties outside KZN, contesting that of the intellectuals of the NP, the DP and a host of think tanks.

At Codesa, the universalist principles, to whose authority the progressive intellectuals appealed, overwhelmed the sectional and ethnicised values espoused by their white supremacist counterparts. In the international community, too, the white racist regime had been stripped of every shred of legitimacy. But, impressive though it was, we can all agree that what was won at the negotiating table was only a partial victory. It created the political conditions to strive for 'a better life for all'.

The success of Codesa, followed by the 1994 elections, represented the transfer of political power to the democratic majority – inclusive of South Africans of every race and class, but dominated by the Black majority. In 1994, the white supremacist and racist minority – whose domination had been sustained by generations of white intellectuals, technocrats and administrators whose ideas lent it legitimacy and whose skills endowed it with economic and military power – was defeated and lost power. In that respect, one can legitimately refer to the democratic breakthrough as a political revolution. The arrival of South African democracy represented a victory for the oppressed.

The Challenges in Post-Apartheid South Africa

The specific circumstance of an industrial revolution, kick-started by mining, in a colonial country imparted a number of distinctive features rooted in its past to South African capitalism. The capitalist mode of production that arrived with mining had not evolved organically, driven by small entrepreneurs and merchants within a feudal social formation as in Europe. It was imposed by imperialist cannon and bayonets in the hire of advanced foreign capitalist interests allied to local capital. Within a decade, it had acquired high levels of monopoly concentration, particularly in the mining-finance complex. It leeched off the pre-capitalist modes of production with which it articulated in South Africa and its hinterland to reproduce the proletariat. It harnessed the institutions, laws and mores of a colonial society as its principal instruments for disciplining the proletariat for capital accumulation. An intricate dialectic of race, colour and class that impacted on every facet of South African capitalism, even post-apartheid, thus evolved.

The template on which South African capitalism was built remains largely unchanged. In the baggage of that unaltered template come all the vices of 'colonialism of a special type' (CST). That volatile mix of contradictions boiled over at Marikana on 16 August 2012.

Addressing a mining lekgotla that same year, then Deputy President Kgalema Motlanthe said, inter alia:

> *Sadly, mining has remained a prisoner of its apartheid past in its core element of cheap labour sourced through a migrant's punishing annual work cycle and the social evils associated with that cycle. No amount of employment equity plans and empowerment transactions have ventured to tamper with this...*

The challenge is devising a developmental path that will result in a decisive break with CST and grow the economy in a manner that will not only develop our productive forces but also reconfigure the racial/class/gender relations bequeathed us by apartheid. Government policy has wrestled with that challenge since 1994. The progressive intellectuals who serve in the institutions of state have been at the rock face of that struggle.

What role, then, do the intellectuals who operate outside the state institutions assign themselves in defining South Africa's developmental path?

During the darks days of apartheid, it was, ironically, the policies of 'separate development' that gave Black intellectuals access to the universities. Before the establishment of the 'bush colleges', outside of Fort Hare, the number of Black academics on university faculties could be numbered on one hand. That newly acquired access, however, also had its own ironic consequences: as when Jakes Gerwel sought to make the University of the Western Cape (UWC) 'the home of the left'. It was, in large measure, in the context of such ironies that the question arose:

Is capitalism the only viable developmental course South Africa can follow?

The historically Black universities became sites of radical and liberation politics after the late 60s. But that ferment was largely among the student body.[2] Through intense debate within student bodies and active participation in mass struggles, the majority adopted the political tradition, values and principles nurtured by the radical intellectuals. Today, those are the hegemonic values and ideas and are the basis of our Constitution and our democratic system. Political discourse is conducted within that tradition and framed by those values. Not unreasonably, progressive intellectuals give serious consideration to criticism coming from the adherents to that democratic value system rather than from its known opponents.

Since the arrival of democracy, progressive Black intellectuals have been forced onto the back foot and made to feel defensive about their political preferences and affiliations.[3] A mantra, speaking truth to power, has become the expected and accepted norm. Any intellectual who refuses to submit to this diktat is dismissed as an 'apologist for the "ruling party"'. An intellectual who openly aligns her or himself with the governing party is dismissed as unworthy of that title. The only 'legitimate' intellectual engagement is that which is oppositional to, or, at the very least, critical of the government and its policies.[4]

There is great merit in intellectuals' capacity to critically distance themselves from the object of their study or observation. Dispassionate study of every dimension of our lives is central to the role of the intellectual. Emotional detachment enhances the ability to rigorously interrogate what is unfolding. So is a willingness to change an opinion on the basis of contrary evidence. All serious intellectual engagement requires a high degree of 'agnosticism' about everything.

Democracy institutionalised the principle of political contestation and the right to be critical. Having won the argument about the direction our country should take – a united, but diverse South Africa – the champions of the vision sketched by Olive Schreiner are now called upon to flesh it out by paving the road to 'a better life for all'. In practice, that raises the question of how progressive intellectuals relate to our democratic institutions, the democratic state and the democratic government.

Towards a Conclusion

Three years ago, addressing the National Association of Democratic Lawyers (NADEL) on the Protection of Information Bill, I told my audience that, as a constituent of the Mass Democratic Movement that had brought democratic change to the country, I had expected NADEL to be amongst the first out of the starting gates on the issue: to engage the democratic government, not as its opponents, but *as critical supporters pursuing essentially the same objectives*, warning the government about those elements of the bill that subverted those shared democratic objectives.

In historic terms, whatever mistakes it has made and will make, the democratic government is *attempting to breathe life into what has, for the passed century, been the political agenda and vision of South Africa's progressive intellectuals.* Should the progressive intelligentsia then not enter the lists as in principle supporters of that *project*, without surrendering their obligations to critically examine and interrogate the manner in which that vision is being pursued? The democratic state, warts and all, is the outcome of the struggles the progressive intellectuals of our country waged on the intellectual, ideological and political terrains. It is by rigorous pursuance of the democratic tradition from which it derives that they can fully appropriate it, defend it, and where necessary, improve it.

There is a distinction between partisanship and partiality. The partisan of a particular cause is not a mindless, uncritical political fan. The partisan has chosen her or his side, but maintains an open mind that assesses and judges issues on their merits, and governments on their performance. The partisan might be a supporter, but one who retains critical faculties and defends the political space for critical and oppositional engagement.

The struggle of Franz Fanon's *Wretched of the Earth* has made impressive gains since the end of World War II. But none of these struggles has yet produced a society in which the quest for freedom has not been compromised for the sake of the struggle for bread. When it assumed political office in 1994, the South African liberation movement undertook to pursue these two objectives in tandem.

I, too, conclude my remarks with a question: What role do the progressive intellectuals wish to play in assisting us to align those two objectives?

End Notes

1. Forced to abandon the ideas and values inherited from precolonial times after the collapse of the economies of the independent African kingdom, the Black intellectuals embraced the universalist concepts derived from Christianity and liberal democratic politics. The second source of universalism was socialism, to which growing numbers of Black radical intellectuals subscribed after 1928.

   Contrasting three policy documents adopted during the 40s most clearly expresses the gulf in the social and political visions of Black and white intellectuals. *The Africans' Claims* (1943) speaks of a united South Africa in which all enjoy equal rights. *The Report of the Fagan Commission on Native Affairs* (1946), inspired by the white liberals, was at best an attempt to come to terms with the reality of African urbanisation. The *Report of the Sauer Commission* (1947), the intellectual product of Afrikaner intellectuals, was the blueprint for apartheid.

2. There is compelling evidence that some Black academics sold out their students; that others actively participated in isolating and persecuting radical students. Even at the radical-led UWC of the 1980s, the role of Black academics was uneven. The teachers' organisations, too, with one or two exceptions, tended to be cautious when not outright conservative. The organised bodies led by the educated that took liberation politics on board were those of independent professionals and the churches.

3. A most disturbing expression of this was the deafening silence of progressive and Black intellectuals after Goldman and Sachs published *Two Decades of Freedom* in 2014, indicating that, though they had not turned the world upside down, *the policies of the governing party had actually changed the lives of the majority of South Africans for the better*. Black intellectuals should have been at the forefront of those dissecting and assessing that report as an account of the changes wrought principally in the lives of their own communities

4. An unnecessary but politically convenient conflation of 'partisanship' and 'partiality' has been injected into South African political discourse. The assumption being that one who is partisan is necessarily partial. Thus we find a situation in which virtually *every daily newspaper – exercising their untrammelled constitutional right –* positions itself as oppositional to the government. Yet, these very same newspapers refuse to *recognise the right of another newspaper to exercise its untrammelled right to support the governing party*. Somehow, that is cast as morally suspect by the others. When it first hit the streets, *The New Age* was treated in this fashion. Cape Town's two dailies, now under new editors, receive the same treatment. Regrettably, Black editors, whom one assumed knew better, have fallen into line behind this dangerous anti-democratic logic. Democracy institutionalises *the right to oppose, alongside the right to support* a political party of one's choice.

Academy-based Feminist Intellectuals and the Nexus of State, Globalisation and Civil Society – Desiree Lewis

As feminists from several traditions have shown, the most powerful feminist intellectual work has come from visionaries, iconoclasts and artists – those who transcend established institutions and forms for scholarship to create knowledge provocations resonating across geographical boundaries with the enduring power to compel and uplift. The poetry and short essays of Audre Lorde, for example, will continue to inspire critical interrogations of networks of power, as well as radical visions of social and personal change.

Despite the dubious and ambivalent role of universities in knowledge-making, I focus on the academy as a site of current challenges around feminist intellectual influence. On the one hand, as several critics have stressed, universities play pivotal roles in the selection and socialisation of elites. They have, therefore, been sites for social reproduction – irrespective of the efforts of individual departments, academics or the ethos of particular universities. On the other hand, universities have been, and remain, influential sites for generating new political registers and frameworks around wide-ranging social and cultural concerns, for influencing public discourses about what kinds of knowledge matter, as well as for shaping knowledge-making among successive generations of graduates who eventually enter several areas in public life.

Exploring the pressures on, and possibilities for, university-based feminist intellectuals, who consistently assert their commitment to social change rather than reproduction, is therefore especially significant in South Africa's

110

present. At a stage when many lament the impoverishment of intellectual thought and the urgent need for critical public debates around, for example, xenophobia, racial transformation, public history, as well as explicitly gendered dynamics such as pervasive and normalised social violence, reflecting on what feminists have to offer and what constrains these interventions is crucial.

African Feminist Intellectuals, Critical Knowledge and the State

Much discussion of the role of academy-based intellectuals in South Africa and the continent more generally focuses on developments within Africa. Emphasis has been placed on the ethical imperative of intellectuals to challenge neo-imperial injustices, as well as their need to retain autonomy from neocolonial and authoritarian governments and state engineering through nation-building and structural adjustment.

Alerting us to the consequences of not doing so, Paul Zeleza (2004) notes that African universities are sites where donor funding, state authoritarianism and market-driven skills entrench a deep acquiescence in universities' intellectual cultures. The current fixation with techno-scientific knowledge, the normalising of academics' moonlighting as 'consultants', instrumentalised knowledge in the service of "'nation-building'" and "'development'" both mirror and reproduce technologies of state-driven priorities and neoliberal governance.

Pursuing a related argument in South Africa, William Gumede and Leslie Dikeni argue that:

> Since 1994, there has been a decline in the vibrancy of intellectual engagement within the ANC and within the society as whole. Debate has been narrowed and dissent discouraged. Many of the leading intellectuals have now become politicians or work in the civil service and the rest have remained in policy think-tanks or universities, mostly focusing on policy research (2009: 9).

Key arguments in their collection of essays reveal that the quality of intellectual thought, whether emanating from NGOs, independent research sites, trade unions or universities has steadily declined (see Gumede and Dikeni, 2009, 1–11).

Intellectual work on gender and sexuality has not been immune to the instrumentalising that Gumede and others identify. African feminist scholar

Charmaine Pereira (2004), argues that deeply constraining forces affect gender research in African contexts so that, despite its current growth, it has increasingly veered towards social reproduction rather than social transformation. First, the perceived imperative of servicing the state leads many researchers to validate government departments' projects in genres such as reports. These convey little about their own passions and politics nor those of women's movements in civil society. Secondly, the reliance on foreign donor support prioritises Western-centric and elite imperatives as well as ameliorative intellectual work through, for example, policy recommendations. This conservatism often overrides critical perspectives with the potential to radically destabilise the status quo. Thirdly, the emphasis on vocational education fosters teaching and methods of student recruitment geared towards training students to slot into the labour market in various sectors, rather than towards critical literacy and equipping graduates with the confidence, theoretical insight and political focus for making interventions.

I believe that it is timeous to deepen Pereira's diagnosis in a way that encourages feminists to grapple courageously with current and emerging challenges. In so doing, we are more likely to transcend disillusionment and defeatism with a renewed sense of the vitality that feminist knowledge-making has to offer. As I suggest in what follows, grappling boldly means squarely confronting a matrix of coercion and co-option in the knowledge economy vortex as the current lynchpin of neoliberal governance and state power. This vortex is not only regional or national; rather, it pervades a globalised world in which knowledge, knowledge capital and human potential are increasingly homogenised in the interests of rampant global capitalism manifested both in relationships and in ethical values and morality.

Global Forces and University-based Intellectuals

Scholars repeatedly remind us of the potential of the humanities in maintaining a critical role for universities and university teaching. Shortly before his death, Jakes Gerwel, one of South Africa's best-known public intellectuals, stressed his absolute confidence in the humanities both in the anti-apartheid struggle and post-apartheid transformation (see Higgins, 2013). This role, Gerwel (Higgins, 2013) suggests, transcends the mere inclusion of social justice critique into social transformation practices and principles; it entails invigorating public debate and education – both in and beyond institutions – in ways that actively shape values, practises and beliefs among a country's inhabitants; in other words, ways that change the 'deep culture, ideologies and mentalities of our political culture' (Gramsci, 2001: 12).

John Higgins (2013) draws attention to the way that humanities teaching extends these effects. Equating substantive academic freedom with robust and rigorous scholarship and teaching in the humanities, he shows that the drive towards economic efficiency, material productivity and economic development is progressively whittling away critical studies of culture, history and text/language/discourse in a higher education environment obsessed with vocational training and bolstering neoliberal capitalist productivity and governance.

Dealing with developments throughout Africa, Stephen Arnold (1990) pursues this argument by showing how rigorous study of human subjectivities and experiences has been 'Balkanised' by technologies and industries of Development Studies. These, he writes: 'are technocratic in nature; they tend to treat humans as cyphers and often regard concrete problems as abstractions calling for technical solutions (1990: vii).' He contrasts this with forms of study that 'are humanistic ... fully accepting the significance of human subjectivity in almost every single human event' (1990: viii). As these writers indicate, the shift towards intellectual work that services developmentalism, nation-building and neocolonial state agendas has been occurring alongside the marginalising of humanities scholarship that is often seen as 'soft', as self-indulgent and as irrelevant.

Critiques of trends in Africa echo several decades of scrutinising the beleaguered place of the humanities in the global North. Two of the key radical intellectuals who have done this are Stuart Hall (1990) and Terry Eagleton (2010). Rooted in their engagement with social justice issues in Britain during massive liberalisation under Thatcher, these scholars show how the cauterising of the humanities has been integral to the efficacy of the neoliberal project: the creation of market-driven knowledge and skills devoid of the philosophical and theoretical legacies, tools, research cultures and public discourses that enable critical responses to the status quo. Universities have increasingly become sites for supporting the status quo rather than spaces for generating imaginative and animated scholarship, teaching and talk about justice, freedom, philosophy, the arts and literature.

It is in some ways disturbing that critiques of the erosion of the humanities are often outraged condemnations of their marginalisation in higher education planning and funding. For example, Premesh Lalu (2012) and John Higgins (2013) remind us in great detail that South African universities – as intricate agents and repositories of neoliberal practice and ideology – are steadily eroding deep explorations of human subjectivities and, alongside growing support for the hard sciences and applied social sciences, are stifling humanities research through market-orientated trajectories of teaching and research.

Such critiques, however unintentionally, suggest a nostalgia for the lost freedoms of universities, although the 'freedoms' of universities have always been hostile to women (especially Black women), to racialised others, and to knowledge-making from the global South. There is a tendency in such arguments to elevate liberal[1] understandings of universities and to ignore the extent to which these earlier liberal notions, while countenancing 'academic freedom' for some, have often entrenched masculinist, Western-centric, elitist biases in the name of 'universality'.

A more difficult step in seeking to revitalise the humanities would involve interrogating exactly what the reasons and implications of its erosion are, as well as what forms of humanities scholarship truly encourage university-based teaching and research as free and critical inquiry. This kind of scrutiny would also mean confronting present institutional dynamics, not as external forces constraining hapless academics, students and university administrators, but as diffuse forms of power that recruit academics and students as active participants in liberal and neoliberal projects. As Margaret Thornton (2009) reminds us, academics, including feminist academics, have become 'active subjects' in the new regimes, and feminist intellectuals often do respond in the form of implicit compliance and accommodation.

In the following section, I survey some of the ways in which current work in the academy reflects the embedded symptoms of the neoliberal and neo-imperial corporatising and management of universities. I suggest that there is evidence of a downward spiral even within humanities and feminist work. Interrupting this trend will require considerable effort, courage and risk.

Neoliberalism, the Knowledge Economy and Feminist Intellectuals

At face value, the growing body of work on gender, sexuality and feminism in Africa augurs well for its persistence as a beleaguered yet resilient site for critical knowledge production and teaching. Yet, there is much about recent work on gender and feminism, and much about how feminist intellectuals situate themselves within the academy that is discouraging. It is worth unravelling the embedded layers of managerialism in our current higher education environment and procedures to understand how corrosive and debilitating recent forms of accommodation to power have been.

One manifestation of this is the co-opting of feminist scholarship and teaching to tie in with bureaucratic control and numerous auditing technologies. Here the proliferation of regulating mechanisms – functioning coercively through promises of rewards and threats of ostracisation – shifts the focus away from academics retaining authority over their own work and the work of peers towards an audit regime revolving around surveillance and homogenisation. Within this regime, academics, including feminist academics, are often enlisted to police one another. In South Africa, these mechanisms include bodies such as the Council on Higher Education and the National Research Foundation. The NRF offers academics considerable rewards on the basis of their submitting to its auditing procedure in the first place, and also conforming to its technicist procedures for individual rating, a primary basis for promotion and appointment. Especially insensitive to the intellectual value of humanities and interdisciplinary feminist work that straddles boundaries and refuses inherited norms of 'field excellence', the NRF rigidly grades research outputs and the standing of individual academics. It therefore locks academics into schemas that pay little attention to the merits of robust and rigorous intellectual thought.

The impact and force of the work of a feminist intellectual such as Patricia McFadden, who over several years has regularly written for regional and international progressive periodicals, magazines and newspapers, would simply not register in the NRF's criteria for academic influence and merit. And this would be the case despite the fact that McFadden has, among other interventions, launched the first African feminist exploration of gender, racial dynamics and HIV and AIDS in southern Africa, produced pioneering studies of how a gender research industry has watered down feminist intellectual thought in Africa, and regularly pursued a transnational perspective in her work on feminism and global struggles for justice long before the popularising of ideas about 'transnational feminism'.

Another dimension to the regulation of university-based academics is an increasingly aggressive and obfuscatory system of 'output accreditation', one that often judges publications associated with vibrant feminism as mediocre, and elevates even the most tedious articles as valuable. The status of the essay, for example, a genre that encourages exciting, imaginative and innovative insight, has steadily been devalued in favour of the technically slick but often mundane 'scholarly article'.

The privileging of this form goes hand in glove with the promotion of 'marketable' sectoral research areas. In terms of this, laborious but 'thoroughly researched' empiricist investigation of examples of gender-based violence could be deemed more valuable than a provocative interdisciplinary analysis of how violence pervades the fabric of our society. As Thornton (2009) has observed, valuable knowledge in the new knowledge economy is increasingly defined as data, rather than as wisdom, and it is data that has come to constitute an untapped source of wealth in terms of market logics. The brittle information often conveyed by the scholarly article is likely to be seen as rational, focused and valuable as 'potentially applicable' research. In contrast, the essay would be considered diffuse, scattered and having no real 'rational' or 'use' value. Regulation and reward mechanisms have therefore increasingly promoted both data and information generation and sectoral work in niche areas. This threatens to supplant the provocative critical work that opens up debate and contestation that threatens to destabilise, rather than support market logic.

Regulation and reward systems have been taken up very swiftly by many academics, students and universities, a terrifying reminder of how the 'market has entered the soul of the university' (Thornton, 2009: 3), and of how poor a fight academics have put up to defend their autonomy. The aggressive ethic of survival of the fittest seems to be seen as the only way to thrive in academies. Few academics have the courage or stamina to pursue what feminism has always needed to pursue: namely, to take risks; to risk the security, not only of jeopardising tenure and promotion, but the security of attaining prestige and authority in the corporatised, technicist and masculinist milieu of the newly 'engaged' university.

Another way in which unbridled neoliberalism affects feminist scholarship is the growing individualism and competitiveness among university-based intellectuals. It would be naïve to suggest that universities have ever encouraged egalitarian and communalistic forms of knowledge production. As elite institutions that carefully regulate a particular person's merit, universities have historically encouraged exclusivity, individualism and competition. But the present emphasis on outputs, achievements and productivity under the new audit culture encourages unbridled and ruthless competitiveness.

As Alan Burton-Jones argues: 'Capitalism and emerging knowledge capitalism thrive on capital accumulation, open-market competition, free trade, the power of the individual and survival of the fittest' (1999: 3). The overwhelming worldly pressure to 'succeed', to be counted and to be 'recognised' in the university system, often supersedes any impulse to create thoughtful and critical knowledge. The rise of social media may contribute significantly to this, since it can increase the value of celebrity intellectuals whose worth is often measured by, for example, the frequency with which they appear on television or produce punchy sound bytes of information, rather than by the vigour of sustained arguments or analysis.

The progressive uses to which new media have been and can be put by feminist intellectual activism are immeasurable. At the same time, it is at great cost to feminist political and intellectual integrity that these platforms are uncritically embraced. In the absence of careful reflection on how they can frame, reconstruct and disseminate knowledge, they can be conscripted by a knowledge economy whose express purpose is to flatten and simplify, to narrowly instrumentalise knowledge in the service of quick-fix closure, and to blunt, rather than to activate, critical public discourse in civil society. The formulaic language of the celebrity intellectual or specialist can implicitly reinforce systems of global neoliberal governance in which information is processed as digestible sound bytes, segments of information that can be quickly registered and then forgotten. Thus, among many who are strategically placed to influence public debate, the recent xenophobic attacks in South Africa have been met by simplistic moralising of others' Afrophobia. Blog essays, tweets and Facebook postings have therefore avoided the searching analysis of post-apartheid South African public history, the entrenchment of racism and compromise after 1994, and the new government's abdication of responsibility to the poor. In contrast to these sorts of complexities, much social media talk reveals a simplistic denunciation of Afrophobia among those 'out there', as though we were not living in a country where, in fact, Afrophobia is routinely naturalised by, for example, the disparaging attitude that many influential (white and Black) academics have towards scholarship from Africa, the attitudes of many middle-class Black and white people to travelling to African countries beyond South Africa, the deeply embedded idea that South Africa is not 'quite African' and is in many ways exceptional.

Similarly, the hugely complex debates about power, intersectionality, class, patron-clientalism and Western-centricism that the 'Rhodes Must Fall' campaign initiated at the University of Cape Town generated disappointingly flat position-taking on social media, rather than a necessary unravelling of class, complicity, co-optation and the inevitably disparate political agendas of middle-class Black students, Black feminists and Black workers at universities.

Globally and continentally, feminist epistemologies and teaching rigorously question social and personal relations and identities, pushing back boundaries around relationships, values, epistemologies and arguments set in place both by overt authoritarianism and by prevailing 'common sense'. Immediate challenges often require radical intellectuals to make quick responses. But radicalism can easily be compromised when individuals seem motivated primarily by the voracious impulse to enter into and acquire visibility in public debates, and so fall short of framing or posing difficult questions, interrupting consensual ideas, and generating the discomfort (both for others and for themselves) that comes from truly taking risks.

A further area in which the potential for radical humanities work has been eroded is teaching. Feminist traditions, including feminist popular education and the links made between academic feminism and popular education, have long pioneered innovative methods for encouraging critical literacy among students. Both popularised and academy-based feminist education connects the intellect, the body, the spirit and the emotions, contesting separations that have traditionally reproduced exclusions, silencing and marginalisation in knowledge-making and teaching. Globally, feminist educators have also experimented boldly with creativity, active learning, and the use of students' knowledges in challenging elite and masculinist forms of education.

In South Africa, feminist popular education has a long history in the work of feminist activists working for NGOs and trade unions. Drawing on the philosophy of the Brazilian educator, Paulo Freire, this work has enlisted traditions of popular education, specifically feminist pedagogies that establish the personal as political, and challenge hegemonic epistemologies and patriarchal claims to universality.

In fact, the University of the Western Cape has been an influential site for this work, having housed the Centre for Continuing and Adult Education (Cace), which drove critical literacy programmes for adults whose social marginalisation constrained their educational goals. Like other radical teaching sites, Cace not only sought to 'prepare students academically', instead it supported students' critical engagement with their worlds, preparing them to challenge local, interpersonal and global injustice, and the ways in which governments and market economies safeguarded minority privileges. It is an indication, not only of the direction taken by this particular university but also others in South Africa, that the University of the Western

Cape, alongside its pursuit for a market-orientated form of 'social engagement', recommended the closure of Cace[2] on the grounds of its no longer being relevant to the institution's educational priorities.

In tandem with this, enormous financial and academic resources went into transforming 'teaching and learning' into a new site for professionalism and regulation. Apart from the employment of full-time staff for overseeing teaching and learning in all departments and faculties, the university appoints Teaching and Learning Deputy Deans in several faculties, and considerable energy and resources have been invested in managerial strategies for 'enhancing' this 'new field'. Long-established academics, with excellent track records of innovative teaching, are now required to submit elaborate teaching portfolios or attend training sessions to qualify for promotion.

It is profoundly disturbing that the new teaching and learning expertise offers far less than the rich, animated, organic and impassioned pedagogical explorations that many feminists, humanities teachers and popular educators have pursued in and beyond South Africa. And it is equally disturbing that the new 'field' has selectively used (and diluted) rich pedagogical traditions that include popular education in South America, adult education in South Africa and feminist teaching in both the North and the South. None of these earlier progressive traditions countenance the authoritarianism implicit in distinguishing between 'teaching' and 'learning'; in fact, codifying 'education' as 'teaching and learning' explicitly entrenches the belief that 'learners' lack knowledge and require instruction, whilst 'teachers' own knowledge and the authority to impart it.

Ultimately, the new technologies for teaching and learning operate within broader bureaucratic systems of managerialism, auditing, and student regulation.[3] And faculty, infrastructure and resources have been mobilised in burgeoning university bureaucracies that now work to micro-manage teaching under the guise of 'quality control and assurance'. (Generally, the language of the market in universities' new technologies speaks volumes about their new lines of accountability.) Unless the lively traditions of popular and feminist education are reactivated and energised, the future of education in South African universities promises to be shaped by technocratic monitoring.

The surveillance, regulation and management of teaching has also been manifested in postgraduates' training. Academics and university departments are constantly enjoined to generate the 'throughput' of postgraduates. Traditionally, the mission of universities has been to undertake research and to teach. More recently, with the emphasis on a 'third mission' for universities, emphasis has been placed on harnessing university teaching to the academy's direct engagement with society and industry. Clearly, the ideal of universities' increased social engagement is a noble and positive one. It promises to deepen academy-based intellectual engagement with civil society and the generation of vibrant public discourse. But the call for a third mission for universities has come not from progressive and transformative agendas, but from a neoliberal quest to exploit knowledge as a new source of wealth creation. The preparation of graduates for 'employment' has therefore concentrated on vocationalism, with so-called 'research universities' now making little distinction in their vision and mission statements or publicity from sites of tertiary-level vocational training.

Currently, the emphasis has been on measuring throughput primarily in quantitative terms, so that the energy and time required to mentor and encourage students as critical and independent knowledge producers has been neglected. This is especially evident in how postgraduates in the social sciences and humanities are currently being encouraged to pursue research. The popularising of theses and research proposals in terms of graduates using a formula (including a theoretical and conceptual framework section, a literature review section, a methodology section, followed by one chapter on findings – often linked to implications for development or society) – is an especially grotesque manifestation of the call to encourage applied research. It is alarming that much postgraduate work on gender and sexuality is currently being produced in terms of this formula, one that stifles independent thought and integrated arguments, and that encourages technicist work that often confirms what is already known or anticipated.

Reinvigorating the Humanities and Feminist Thought

The intellectual climates of many African universities and others in the Black diaspora were initially marked by animated conversations around the humanities and especially literary studies. Robust debates were generated by the work of humanities scholars and poets including Leopold Senghor, Aime Cesaire, Edouard Glissant, Chinua Achebe, Wole Soyinka, Ngugi wa Thiongo, Eskia Mphahlele and Njabulo Ndebele. These figures, many of whom have been poets and fiction-writers, shaped intellectual cultures and political ideas about the public good that reverberated beyond the university.

Currently, intellectual work in African universities has become terrifyingly conformist, uncritical and mundane. Attributing this solely to external forces, such as the power of the state or the authority of global surveillance cannot take us very far, since the success of the system has rested on the manufacture of consent, on ensuring that universities and academics manage themselves within the new knowledge economy regime.

It is noteworthy that the hierarchy that this regime has currently put into place, one disparaging the humanities as irrational, soft and dispensable, is a gendered one.[4] This gendering of the intellectual landscape is revealing about the challenges that disparaged knowledges pose. As a zone that has been reviled and ghettoised, critical humanities scholarship has a similar potential force and power to feminist subject matter. Even as it is vilified and marginalised, the fear of what it can lay bare, destabilise and unsettle remains. And the response of managers, certain academics, administrators and education policymakers is to contain, regulate and sideline the threat.

What would it mean to revitalise humanities teaching and research from the perspective of feminist thought and knowledge-making – given the seemingly overwhelming system in which governmentality works, not only to maintain the status quo, but to assure all subjects within it that the status quo is inevitable, rational and just? One important route is for feminist intellectuals to undertake courageous, self-reflexive critiques, not only of where they are currently situated, but of their own complex relations of dependence, co-dependence and complicity with the embedded hierarchies and technologies of management and self-management in the academy. Such self-assessment would entail questioning collective stakes in their comfort and security zones, the complex and layered investments they make in affiliation and disaffiliation, the dangers of speaking out and stepping out of line. These are the kinds of challenges that generations of feminist intellectual activists have urged within, and especially outside, of the academy.

Alongside this kind of self-reflexivity is the value of rebuilding research communities that have traditionally strengthened feminism. By this I do not mean the opportunistic bonds among women scholars that often reinforce patriarchal forms of patronage, authoritarianism, mentorship and obedience. All too frequently, these ensure that a minority of powerful women gain 'recognition' and 'respect' on the backs of others. Nor am I referring to the support groups that, while seemingly necessary in addressing the erosion experienced under patriarchal and racist academic regimes, often create ghettoised comfort zones by distorting our sense of ourselves, our work and our 'commonality'. Rather, I am endorsing an energising sense of feminist community where nourishing relations of contestation, debate, argument and personal and intellectual growth strengthen our critical sense of ourselves and where we can go.

Among recent feminists based in the corporatised academy, Jacqui Alexander and Chandra Mohanty (2010) have provided especially compelling discussions and explanations of radical networking. They have argued that the following are central questions within new radical transnational networks: 'What are the specific challenges for collaborative transnational feminist praxis given the material and ideological sites that most of us occupy? And what forms of struggle engenders cultures of dissent and decolonised knowledge practices in the context of radical transnational feminist projects? (2010: 26)' It is ironic that the cult of individualism generated by the new knowledge economy often leaves individual feminist intellectuals extremely vulnerable, isolated, fragile and battered. It is not surprising that Black feminists in the South African academy especially have suffered tremendous physical, emotional and psychological distress. Few things can replace the sense of security, power, vitality and confidence that feminist networks can create.

A third area where feminism can invigorate the stifling impasse in academy-based knowledge creation and teaching is in subject matter. It is wearying and demoralising to find that feminist journals, seminars and conferences return with unfailing regularity to familiar and well-trodden ground: for example, sexualities, teaching and learning, HIV and Aids and gender, gender-based violence, gender mainstreaming and citizenship.

Paradoxically, this constant revisiting of 'gender themes' entails feminist academics living up to the expectation of their appropriate and 'relevant' reproductive roles in the new knowledge economy. Since one need of this economy is how to manage social crises such as HIV and Aids, gender-based violence and overt evidence of inequality and social injustice, the revisiting of sectoralised social problems, such as violence against women, or gender disparities in politics and higher education, conveniently compartmentalises feminist work. Implicitly or explicitly constructed as ancillary servicing fields, sectoral feminist work – irrespective of the intentions of researchers – guarantees the efficient productivity of our newly instrumentalised knowledge economy. This work's servicing role revolves around the care, welfare and support functions that neoliberal universities need – on the one hand to demonstrate a token concern with social challenges, and on the other to absolve institutions and academics as a whole from collectively engaging with social justice challenges. Feminist work is therefore ghettoised as reproductive work.

Certain kinds of feminist work can also be co-opted for obviously conservative ends. For example, the abundant work on violence against women in the global South can often reinforce the racial othering of certain women as perpetual victims. As Hester Eisenstein (2010) has argued, it can confirm the neo-imperial myth that gender and sexual minorities in 'other cultures' require rescue by the West – even if this includes the violence of the 'war on terror'. Irrespective of the forceful ways in which these subjects might be pursued, sectoral work devoid of cross-cutting and holistic attention to power, can function to stabilise the status quo. Unless their consequences are interrogated and integrated into knowledge production, the objects and effects of certain kinds of work on gender and sexuality can recycle and confirm particular power dynamics.

Currently, the pervasive bureaucratisation and surveillance entrenched in the academy seem so terrifying that academics, including feminist academics, simply dare not step out of line. Yet, thinking through, for example, the historical and contextual implications of human sexualities, might entail a very rigorous exploration of what heterosexuality has meant and how it has been coerced – and so interrupt the hegemonic compartmentalising of knowledge fields in ways that atomised work on, for example, non-normative sexualities does. Or the familiar feminist forays into politics and leadership might push back the boundaries around this field to explore how, alongside the gendered power structure that exists 'out there' as expressions of gender injustice, all socially constructed subjects are enjoined to take up positions in a gendered and heterosexualised hierarchy, or risk exclusion, punishment or ostracisation.

Lastly, despite significant amounts of feminist work on higher education, it seems to me that an ongoing challenge for feminists would be to undertake a radical analysis of what the new patriarchal corporatising and auditing of universities is doing to the production of critical knowledge. While existing feminist qualitative studies of the HE environment are informative and insightful, it may require bolder analysis to confront just what it means to fully grapple with what the new status quo is doing, and how it works.

An array of linked subjects deserves and needs feminist attention. These linked subjects may not fall into categories approved by the NRF or by the various donor, university or government-funded projects that guarantee our research moneys or support for our graduate students. But they are areas that we must, if we are to be honest with ourselves, pursue with passion, with courage and with integrity.

References

Alexander, J. and Mohanty, C. 2010. 'Cartographies of Knowledge and Power: Transnational Feminism as Radical Praxis', Swarr and Nagar, R. (eds.), *Critical Transnational Feminist Praxis*. Albany: State University of New York.

Burton-Jones, A. 1999. *Knowledge Capitalism, Business, Work and Learning in the New Economy*. Oxford: Oxford University Press.

Eagleton, T. 2010. 'The Death of Universities' in *The Guardian*.

Eisenstein, H. 2010. *Feminism Seduced: How Global Elites Use Women's Labor and Ideas to Exploit the World*. Boulder, CO: Paradigm.

Gramsci, A. 2011. *Prison Notebooks*. Columbia University Press.

Gumede, W. and Dikeni, L. 2009. *South African Democracy and the Retreat of Intellectuals*. Johannesburg: Jacana.

Hall, S. 1990. 'The Emergence of Cultural Studies and the Crisis of the Humanities', *The Humanities as Social Technology*, 53, 11–23.

Higgins, J. 2013. *Academic Freedom in a Democratic South Africa*. Johannesburg: Wits University Press.

Lalu, Premesh. 2012. 'The Humanities After Apartheid', *Mail & Guardian*, 4 May 2012.

Pereira, C. 2004. 'Locating Gender and Women's Studies in Nigeria: What Trajectories for the Future?' http://www.gwsafrica.org/knowledge/index.html

Thornton, M. 2009. 'Universities Upside Down: The Impact of the New Knowledge Economy', Australia National University College of Law Research Paper, No. 10–13.

Zeleza, P. 2004. 'Neo-liberalism and Academic Freedom' in Zeleza, P. and Olukoshi, A. (eds.) *African Universities in the Twenty-first Century*. Pretoria: Unisa Press.

End notes

1. In contrast to neoliberal preoccupations with defining universities' roles according to the logic of the market, liberal understandings have defined universities as elite enclaves. Classical liberalism protects the academy as a site of free inquiry from state and capital's interference as well as from the marginalised groups who threaten to unsettle the elite's racialised, gendered and regional authority as knowledge-makers.

2. Cace has not closed; however, it has now merged with another centre and its original focus on critical popular education has been significantly weakened.

3. I have dwelt on trends at the University of the Western Cape since I am most familiar with these. But the trends I identify are national. For a revealing indication of these, see a report titled 'Quality Teaching and Learning in South African Universities: Policies and Practices', which calls for a 'broader scope of quality assurance in higher education … leading to a better interface with industry and society' (25). The report was co-written by Fourie, M.; van der Westhuizen, L.; Alt, H. and Holtzhausen, S. based at the Unit for Research into Higher Education at the University of the Free State.

4. I have used this notion elsewhere, but am indebted to Margaret Thornton's discussion of it in the higher education environments in the global North.

CONTRIBUTORS

Nic Wolpe

Nicholas left South Africa in February 1964 to join his parents in the UK. His father, Harold Wolpe, who had been arrested at the end of July 1963, following the raid on Liliesleaf, broke out of Marshall Square prison and went into exile.

Nicholas was educated in the UK and attended Warwick University where he graduated in 1988 with a BA Honours in Sociology and in 1991 returned to South Africa following the family's 27 years in exile.

During the 1990s he worked in the NGO and public sectors and in 1994 he worked on the first democratic elections, where he headed up the Independent Electoral Commission's Special Projects Voter Education Unit.

He is the founder and CEO of the Liliesleaf Trust and is the driving force behind the Liliesleaf Legacy Project, which has preserved, restored and developed a dynamic immersive and interactive exhibit.

For Nicholas, Liliesleaf is more than just a seminal historical site, it is also a site of memory, a place where a seminal period in South Africa's liberation struggle comes alive. He has also published, written and delivered papers on the relevance and importance of memory and the need to keep memory alive.

Dr Mcebisi Ndletyana

As from 1 October 2015, Dr Ndletyana is Associate Professor in the Pan African Institute in the Faculty of Humanities at the University of Johannesburg. At the time of the roundtable, he was the Faculty Head of the Political Economy Faculty at MISTRA. Before joining MISTRA he held research positions at various research institutions, including the Human Sciences Research Council (HSRC), the Centre for Policy Studies (CPS) and the Steve Biko Foundation. He has also held lecturing positions at the Marymount Manhattan College (New York) as well as at the City University of New York's Hunter College. He holds a Ph.D. in political science from the University of the Witwatersrand. Dr Ndletyana's academic and research interests include the history of African intellectualism, memory and identity, nationalism and electoral politics.

Dr Ibbo Mandaza

Ibbo Mandaza is a Zimbabwean academic, author and publisher. He holds a Doctorate of Philosophy (D.Phil.) in Political Economy from the University of York in England (1979) and taught at the Universities of Botswana, Zambia, Dar es Salaam and Zimbabwe (part-time). He has researched and written extensively on issues of governance, international relations and public policy, and was one of the first senior African civil servants in post-independent Zimbabwe (1980–1990), having been a member of the Zimbabwe national liberation movement in the Department of Research, Education and Manpower at ZANU Headquarters in Maputo, Mozambique. He served as director of the National Manpower Survey and permanent secretary in the Ministry of Manpower Planning and Development; as deputy chairman of the Public Service Commission and member of the Defence Forces Commission; and finally as chairman of the Parastatals Commission before his early retirement from the civil service in July 1990 at the age of 42.

Ibbo Mandaza was chairman of the board of directors of the second largest tourism and hotel group (Rainbow Tourism Group) in Zimbabwe from 1992 to 2009.

Ibbo Mandaza is currently executive chairman of the Southern African Political Economy Series (SAPES) Trust, a regional think tank and convenor of the Policy Dialogue Forum.

Dr Ayanda Ntsaluba

Dr Ayanda Ntsaluba was appointed as a group executive director of Discovery Limited in July 2011. He holds a medical degree from the University of Natal, specialised in Obstetrics and Gynaecology, holds an MSc in Health Policy, Planning and Financing from the University of London and an Executive MBA from the Graduate School of Business at the University of Cape Town.

Before joining Discovery, he served as a deputy director-general for Policy and Planning in the National Department of Health from 1995–1998 and as director-general of Health in South Africa from September 1998 to August 2003. In September 2003, Ayanda was appointed director-general of the Department of Foreign Affairs of the Republic of South Africa – a post he held until March 2011.

He currently also serves as a non-executive board member of South African Tourism, a member of The Lancet – University of Oslo Commission on Global Governance for health in collaboration with the Harvard Global Health Institute as well as a member of the board of trustees of the South African National Aids Trust.

Professor Xolela Mangcu

Xolela Mangcu is Associate Professor of Sociology at the University of Cape Town and an Oppenheimer Fellow at the Hutchins Center for African and African American Research at Harvard University. He is the author and co-author of eight books, including the recently published, *Biko: A Biography* (Tafelberg 2012/13), and *Arrogance of Power: South Africa's Leadership Meltdown* (2014). His ninth book, *The Colour of Our Future* (2015), is being published by Wits University Press.

Mangcu was also the founder of the Platform for Public Deliberation and founding executive director of the Steve Biko Foundation. He has held fellowships at the Brookings Institution, Harvard University, the Massachusetts Institute of Technology, and the Rockefeller Foundation.

He obtained his BA and MSc degrees from Wits University and his Ph.D. from Cornell.

Joel Netshitenzhe

Joel Netshitenzhe is the executive director and board vice-chairperson of the Mapungubwe Institute for Strategic Reflection (MISTRA). He has a Master of Science (MSc) degree in Financial Economics and a post-graduate diploma in Economic Principles from the University of London, and a diploma in Political Science from the Institute of Social Sciences in Moscow.

He is a past member of the National Planning Commission and a member of the ANC National Executive Committee. He is also a member of the boards of the Nedbank Group and Life Healthcare Group, and a Champion within Programme Pioneer of the Nelson Mandela Foundation and Life College Association.

Before joining the Government Communication and Information System (GCIS) as CEO in 1998, Mr Netshitenzhe was Head of Communication in President Nelson Mandela's office. In addition to being GCIS CEO, he was appointed Head of the Policy Coordination and Advisory Services (PCAS) in The Presidency in 2001. He headed the PCAS on a full-time basis from 2006 until his retirement in 2009.

Before 1994, he served in various capacities within the ANC: Radio Freedom, *Mayibuye* editor, member of the ANC Politico-Military Council and deputy head of the Department of Information and Publicity, and as part of the ANC negotiating team.

Professor Ben Turok

Professor Ben Turok was a member of Parliament in South Africa until recently, representing the ruling party, the African National Congress. In the 1994 democratic government, he was first Head of the Commission on the Reconstruction and Development Programme (RDP) in the Gauteng Provincial Cabinet and then moved to Parliament in 1995. He was the co-chair of the Committee on Ethics and Members' Interests of both Houses in Parliament. He has been a member of the liberation movement for many decades, was an accused in the 1956 Treason Trial, served three years in prison and was in exile for 25 years, returning in 1990.

Ben Turok has three degrees: in engineering, philosophy and political science. He is the author of 20 books on Africa's development economics and politics, has lectured at many universities across Africa, and presented papers at numerous conferences and seminars including the United Nations and the European Parliamentary Assembly. He taught at the Open University, UK, for many years, the University of Zambia, and is Visiting Professor at the University of KwaZulu-Natal. He has presented papers at many international conferences.

The United Nations Economic Commission for Africa commissioned him to initiate a major study in ten countries on value addition in Africa's natural resources, which was the basis for the Economic Report on Africa 2013. He was a panellist at the experts' conferences preceding the meetings of Ministers of Finance, Planning and Economic Development at Addis Ababa in 2012 and Abidjan in 2013. His most recent book *With My Head Above the Parapet* has received a great deal of media attention.

He is the editor of *New Agenda, South African Journal of Social and Economic Policy*, published by the Institute for African Alternatives of which he is now the full-time director. The Institute is engaged in policy research in partnership with the UNECA and other agencies. It also publishes books from time to time.

Professor Ari Sitas

Professor Sitas is a professor and Head of the Sociology Department at the University of Cape Town, a post he took over in 2009. He also chairs the board of the National Institute for the Humanities and Social Sciences, an institution that was promulgated after his and Sarah Mosoetsa's pioneering work in creating a charter for the fields of study in 2011.

Besides a remarkable academic career, he has been a distinguished poet, writer and dramatist. His selected poems have just been published by Deep South under the title *Rough Music*. His audacious, *Around the World in 80 Days – the India Section* is published by Unisa Press. His poems have been translated into Zulu, French, German, Greek, Turkish, Urdu and Hindi and many have been set to music.

Before his appointment as a professor at UCT he had spent 27 years in Durban where he, his colleagues and collaborators were key to the anti-apartheid and transformation processes that have shifted society from an authoritarian colonial enclave into a democratic and radical space. Such work in cultural, community, cooperative and workplace contexts still resonates as a cultural renaissance. So has the work he and others put in place to move the province from conflict to civility.

Sitas grew up in colonial Cyprus during the island's independence struggles and bi-communal strife and matured in Johannesburg where he received his undergraduate and postgraduate education at Wits. He received his Ph.D. in 1984 under the supervision of Eddie and David Webster.

Any e-search has his name well-correlated with the founding of the workers' and people's theatre movements, Fosatu, Cosatu, Cosaw, Natal Culture Congress, Culture and Working Life Project, Youth Unemployment Projects, the RDP, ANC in KZN, KZN Economic Council, Chris Hani Institute, African Renaissance Development Trust and a plethora of academic leadership positions.

He is increasingly seen as a significant 'Southern theorist' and works actively with African, Latin American and Asian networks to establish, in his own words, a new knowledge commons which is sensitive to all nodal points of this shrinking planet. He is also a South African representative on the BRICS Think Tanks Council.

Professor Tshilidzi Marwala

Professor Tshilidzi Marwala is Deputy Vice-Chancellor of Research at the University of Johannesburg and an independent non-executive director for EOH Holdings. He is a member of the South African Academy of Engineering, the World Academy of Science and South African Academy. He has published eight books on artificial intelligence, supervised 43 Masters and 18 Ph.D. students to completion.

Nomboniso Gasa

Through her work with the Rural Women's Action Research (RWAR), Nomboniso focuses on the intersections, continuities and discontinuities between the past and the present, especially on questions relating to land and customary systems.

Gasa's political life started in her teens, with her first detention without trial at the age of 14. For almost 32 of her 46 years, Gasa has been involved in political and gender struggles in one or other form, including student activism, the political underground and in the women's movements. Gasa worked for the African National Congress's Commission on the Emancipation of Women, through which she was part of the ANC internal and backup team on gender, traditional leadership issues and rural democracy during the negotiations. She served in the Commission for Gender Equality.

Wrestling with the unsaid and unsayable, Gasa is best known for her skill in weaving the academic and her activism into her research, writing and public commentary. Her work continuously interrogates the relationship between power, political issues, gender, masculinities, femininities, land environmental questions and issues of social and political location.

For more than ten years, she worked on the making of a man, masculinities, manhood, initiation and rites of passage. She continues to work on the 'girl child', particularly early marriages and the impact of male rites of passage in parts of the Eastern Cape. She has published in scholarly, commercial and other media.

Gasa is currently working on the study of the body as a site of identity, ritual and manhood. This examines some of the issues that continue to mark South African society today.

As an art critic, she has published essays in catalogues and has written in 'mainstream' media, including for exhibitions relating to manhood, identity and the Shembe church.

Gasa worked in Nigeria for four-and-a-half years, where she represented the International Institute for Democracy and Electoral Assistance. Following the intense consultative process, a substantive report entitled 'Democracy in Nigeria: Continuing Dialogue(s) for Nation Building' was produced.

Professor David Moore

David Moore is Professor of Development Studies at the University of Johannesburg. He has researched and written since the mid-1980s on the history, politics and political economy of Zimbabwe and continues in that vein, along with development theory. His recent publications include 'Conflict and After: Primitive Accumulation, Hegemonic Formation and Democratic Deepening', *Stability: International Journal of Security and Development*, (April 2015) and 'Five Funerals, No Weddings, a Couple of Birthdays: Terry Ranger, his Contemporaries, and the End of Zimbabwean Nationalism, 24 October 2013–3 January 2015', *Review of African Political Economy*, (June 2015); 'An Arc of Authoritarianism in Africa: Toward the End of a Liberal Democratic Dream?' is forthcoming in the 2016 edition of *Socialist Register*.

Z. Pallo Jordan

Z. Pallo Jordan is an ANC veteran who served in various capacities in exile in the 1970s and 80s. In 1975, he worked in the ANC's office in London as a researcher in the Department of Information and Publicity. He was deployed to Luanda, Angola in 1977 to head Radio Freedom and also became involved in training programmes for new recruits to Umkhonto we Sizwe, employing his academic background in history to compile a syllabus for political training.

In 1979, he was appointed director of the ANC's internal mass propaganda campaign, The Year of the Spear, marking the centenary of the Battle of Isandhlwana. In 1980, Jordan was promoted to head the Research Unit of the ANC Department of Information and Publicity in Lusaka, Zambia. He was elected on to the National Executive Committee (NEC) at the Kabwe conference in 1985 and became Secretary of Information of the ANC in 1989.

After South Africa's first democratic elections in April 1994, Jordan served as Minister of Posts, Telecommunications and Broadcasting until 1996, after which he served as Minister of Environmental Affairs and Tourism until 1999. From 1999 to 2004, he served as Chairperson of the Foreign Affairs Committee in the National Assembly. After the 2004 National Elections, Jordan was appointed Minister of Arts and Culture, a post he held until May 2009.

Desiree Lewis

Desiree Lewis has taught literary studies at the Universities of the Witwatersrand, Cape Town, KwaZulu-Natal and the Western Cape. She has also lectured on Women's and Gender Studies at universities in and beyond South Africa. She has a research interest in literary and popular culture, global feminist knowledge and politics, the politics of visuality and representation, and postcolonial writing and culture. She has been a Fulbright scholar-in-residence, a research associate at the Nordic Africa Institute in Uppsala, Sweden and a visiting researcher and lecturer in the United States and Sweden. She currently serves on the editorial boards of four academic journals and is a council member of the National English Literary Museum.

Desiree Lewis has also been active in developing feminist intellectual activist networks throughout Africa, within South Africa and in the Western Cape. She undertook research and editorial work on feminist networking and knowledge production at the African Gender Institute between 2001 and 2003; taught a course on feminist theory and epistemology for postgraduate students in the Zimbabwean-based network, SAPES, between 1993 and 2005; has participated in webinars, workshops and seminars on gender, race and sexualities in South Africa, and produces accessible writings, and mentors new writers' work on feminism and gender. A key activity here involves the NRF's emerging researchers' forum, an online research community platform (See http://ern.nrf.ac.za).

Lewis' intellectual networking includes keynote addresses and guest lectures. Among these are:

- 'Scripted Sexualities in South Africa', public lecture hosted by the Department of Social and Cultural Analysis, New York University, 9 April, 2013.
- 'African Same-Sex Struggles: Development or Utopia?' Keynote address delivered at the *African Same-Sex Sexualities and Diversity Conference* organised by the HSRC, Roodevallei Country Estate, Pretoria, 13–16 February, 2011.
- 'Performative Queering: the Politics of South Africa's Sexual Rights'. Keynote address delivered at 'Desiring Economies/Just Economies of Desire', ICI Berlin Institute for Cultural Inquiry, Berlin, 24–26 June 2010.
- 'Embodying Feminist Resistance: Performance and Self-styling in South Africa'. Keynote address delivered at a conference entitled, *The*

133

Possibilities of Materiality, Abo University, Turku, Finland, 20–22 November 2009.

- 2007: 'Finding the Local in the Global' Keynote address delivered at conference on *Teaching Literature in Georgia State*, English Department, Georgia State University, 8–9 March.

In addition to formal collaborative networks, Desiree Lewis is committed to partnerships for encouraging public debate about feminism, gender, sexuality and race beyond the academy. Partners here have included the feminist journal, *Agenda*, the HSRC, the Gender Equity Unit at the University of the Western Cape and Oxfam Canada.